Higher Education and Corporate Realities

Higher Education and Corporate Realities

Class, culture and the decline of graduate careers

Phillip Brown & Richard Scase

University of Kent at Canterbury

First published in 1994 by UCL Press

UCL Press Limited
University College London
Gower Street
London WC1E 6BT

The name of University College London (UCL) is a registered trade
mark used by UCL Press with the consent of the owner.

ISBN:
1-85728-103-9 HB
1-85728-104-7 PB

British Library Cataloguing in Publication Data
A catalogue record for this book is available from the British Library.

Library of Congress Cataloging-in-Publication Data

Brown, Phillip, 1957–
    Higher education and corporate realities: class, culture and the
decline of graduate careers / Phillip Brown, Richard Scase.
        p.   cm.
    Includes bibliographical references and index.
    ISBN 1-85728-103-9 (HB): $60.00. – ISBN 1-85728-104-7 (PB):
$24.95
    1. College graduates – Employment – United States. 2. Professional
employees – Recruiting – United States. 3. Executives – Recruiting –
United States. 4. Organizational change – United States. 5. Education,
Higher – United States. I. Scase, Richard. II. Title.
HD 6278.U5B76 1994   91-12561
331.11'423–dc20   CIP

Typeset in Plantin.
Printed and bound by
Biddles Ltd., Guildford and King's Lynn, England.

Contents

Authors   vii
Preface   ix
Acknowledgements   x

1 Organizational change and managerial careers   1

2 Education, recruitment and changing patterns
  of cultural reproduction   15

3 Higher education and the regulation of talent   32

4 Social divisions of learning   55

5 Student orientations to work and careers   86

6 The adaptive paradigm and employer
  recruitment strategies   116

7 Graduates in employment: coming to terms
  with changing corporate realities   146

8 Mass higher education and the collapse of
  bureaucratic work?   164

References   181
Index   191

Authors

Phil Brown is a lecturer in Sociology at the University of Kent at Canterbury. He previously worked at the Institute of Criminology, University of Cambridge, and as a craft apprentice at British Leyland, Cowley, Oxford. He has written, co-authored and co-edited a number of books including *Schooling Ordinary Kids* (1987), *Beyond Thatcherism* (1989), *Poor work: disadvantage and the division of labour* (1991), *Education for economic survival* (1992), and *Economic restructuring and social exclusion* (1994). He is currently writing a book, with Hugh Lauder, on education and the global economy.

Richard Scase is Professor of Sociology and Organisational Behaviour at the University of Kent at Canterbury. He is the author of *Social democracy in capitalist society* (1977), *The entrepreneurial middle class* (1982), *Women in charge* (1985), *The real world of the small business owner* (1987), *Reluctant managers* (1989), *Class* (1992) and (with Howard Davis) *Western capitalism and state socialism* (1985). He has edited six volumes and written numerous papers for academic and non-academic books and journals.

Preface

The relationship between higher education and the economy is undergoing fundamental change. There has been a shift from an elite towards a mass system of higher education, where approximately a third of young people can expect to become university students by the year 2000. At the same time, both private and public sector organizations are being restructured in ways that challenge conventional assumptions about managerial and professional careers. Bureaucratic forms of organization are being superseded by alternative structures that are often labelled "flexible" or "adaptive". Accordingly, there is an increasing need for managerial and professional employees with a range of personal competences that extend beyond the exhibition of technical expertise. Therefore, to what extent are the growing numbers of students graduating from university aware of, and how are they responding to, changes in the graduate labour market and work organization? What do students think they have learnt during their time in higher education, and how do they view their chances of finding professional or managerial work in competition with graduates from other universities? To what extent do they subscribe to a meritocratic ideology of academic and occupational success or failure? Will the "adaptive" organization offer greater opportunities for personal self-development or will their "flatter" and "leaner" structures – with the subsequent loss of corporate careers – lead to frustration, disillusionment and continuing divisions in the opportunities available to newly-qualified graduates? These are some of the questions we attempt to answer in this book. Nevertheless, our conclusions must remain tentative in a context of rapid social and economic change and because they are based on a relatively small number of in-depth interviews with students attending three universities, with graduates who had found employment, and with graduate recruiters who have traditionally offered a large number of career opportunities to university graduates.

The idea for this book resulted from discussions between Phil Brown and Richard Scase in 1989. We are grateful to the University of Kent's Research Committee, who provided us with a small grant to undertake a "pilot" study of students' attitudes towards work. Pat Ainley joined the project on a part-time basis in January 1991, funded by Enterprise Kent as part of the Enterprise in Higher Education Initiative. He collected interview data from students at two of the three universities in this study, and was responsible for writing the first drafts of Chapters 3, 4 and 5.

Acknowledgements

We wish to thank Nicola Kerry for her secretarial support during the preparation of this manuscript, Felicity Carlton for her help in collecting data on students, and Christine Daymon, who interviewed graduate recruiters and some of the employed graduates. We are also grateful to Arnold Goldman at Enterprise Kent, John Greer at the University of Kent Careers Advisory Service, and, of course, to all the students and employers who agreed to be interviewed as part of this study.

CHAPTER ONE

Organizational change and managerial careers

The growth of large-scale organizations has been one of the major social trends of the 20th century. In all the industrialized societies, there has been the emergence of multinational corporations that have dominated and shaped the character of domestic economies and the global division of labour (Chandler 1977, Wallerstein 1979). Alongside this process there has been the growth of state institutions as a result of a need to provide services in such areas as education, health, and social welfare (Esping-Andersen 1990). Despite the rediscovered popularity of "enterprise" and "entrepreneurship", state institutions in most of the advanced capitalist economies continue to shape the character of the social structure as well as the economic fabric within which profit-making corporations operate (Burrows 1991). Therefore, it is not surprising that the dominance of large-scale institutions – both in the private and the public sectors – has attracted the attention of social scientists. The emergence of such organized forms raises important issues about patterns of decision-making in society, ownership and control, and social accountability (Kumar 1989). Further, the growth of large-scale organizations has fundamental ramifications for the dynamics of class relationships and, coupled with them, the patterning of opportunity structures. Indeed, no analysis of social class and social mobility in society can be undertaken adequately without consideration being given to the broader processes of organizational change (Scase 1992).

Unfortunately, there are few studies of organizational change that are related to analyses of the dynamics of class relationships and to the distribution of opportunities and rewards in society. A number of factors account for this, not least the fragmentation of sociological research into a number of subdivisions such as "education", "work and organization", "social class and stratification", so that key inter-relationships are neglected because they cut across what have now become *traditional* academic divisions within sociology. Although sociological research in the areas of social class, education, stratification, and social mobility has documented historically and cross-nationally broader social trends, rarely have these been related to specific processes of organizational change and how they, in turn, lead to changing demands for different kinds of human talent (Sabel 1982). Thus there are few sociologically-informed studies of how organizational restructuring is requiring new management competences and offering different kinds of careers with important implications for staff recruitment and training (Constable and McCormick 1987). The lack of such analysis is especially surprising, given that a process of organizational restructuring is currently affecting the nature of managerial work and this, in turn, is leading to changing demands for the "quality" and "nature" of human skills (Handy 1989). The selection of those chosen for employment in large organizations is becoming both more complex and indeterminate because of the growing importance that senior managers attach to intangible personal qualities in their recruitment processes (Scase and Goffee 1989). This is having ramifications for the "providers" of managerial and professional skills, such as institutions of higher education (IHEs). Hence, one of the reasons why corporate leaders claim that higher education is failing to meet the needs of industry in Britain is not because of the precise quality of technical competences which university students acquire, but because of their perceived inability to produce personal qualities considered to be appropriate for newly-emerging paradigms of organization (CBI 1989).

During the immediate postwar decades the prevailing paradigm of organizational design was one that emphasized the desirability of *bureaucracy* and the *bureaucratic* mode of operation.[1] Thus, as organizations expanded, corporate leaders developed systems of administration which were largely based upon *Fordist* methods and principles (Gramsci 1971). As on the shop floor, the ongoing pursuit of cost-effectiveness and rationality was achieved through job fragmentation and the creation of management processes based upon a precisely defined division of work tasks (Braverman 1974). If the principles of

2

Fordism (or scientific management) enabled managers to exercise tight supervisory control over shop floor operatives, it was the opinion of corporate leaders that similar methods could be applied to the execution of middle managerial and administrative work tasks. Accordingly, administrative work processes could be systematically investigated through "scientific" enquiry and, on the basis of detailed analysis of each persons work tasks, rational administrative and managerial work processes could be created (Bendix 1956). It was because of this that the postwar decades witnessed the rapid growth of "management science" as an academic discipline, with its application of the techniques of operational research and systems analysis to management practices.

The outcome was the design of organizations according to a number of core principles, many of which have become synonymous with the notion of bureaucracy as it is conventionally discussed within the sociological literature (Child 1984). Thus the rational and therefore cost effective organization was one in which there was centralized control with hierarchical decision-making. Communication procedures were required to be vertically structured so that those vested with senior managerial authority could monitor and control the flow of information and determine the effective allocation of resources within the organization. The bureaucratic paradigm of organization stressed the need for tasks to be allocated according to strictly defined principles of *superordination* and *subordination*. Hence obedience and compliance were strongly emphasized as organizational values. But equally important was the breakdown of the total work process into precisely defined job tasks. If this was one of the essential features of "Fordist" forms of shop floor organization (Sabel 1982), it was considered just as pertinent for determining the rational allocation of duties among managers with the adoption of bureaucratic forms of control, the potential indeterminacy and ambiguity of managerial work is routinized into co-ordinated and precisely designated job descriptions which become the tasks and duties of individuals. Consequently, a further objective of Fordism can be attained, namely the nurturing of "expert" skills and competences. But as managers undertake their duties within a clearly designated division of tasks, bounded by systems of authority and steeped in relationships of superordination and subordination, they become dependent upon both the organization and each other through rôle allocation in the exercise of their duties. At the same time, a cognitive management style emerges which emphasizes dependency, conformity, co-operation, and "satisfactory" job performance (Merton 1964).

The implications of such assumptions for recruitment procedures are self-evident. The overriding goal is to select those who are prepared to undertake their tasks in a compliant, dutiful, and reliable manner. The required behaviour of middle managers is to perform "satisfactorily" rather than "outstandingly", if only because the latter can lead to uncertainties and therefore ambiguities within the work process. Staff recruitment therefore focuses upon those who can demonstrate an ability to learn the rules, who are prepared to be compliant within rôles of superordination and subordination, and who are able to work with others within a functionally interdependent division of labour. They are not expected to be "creative", "entrepreneurial", or "individualistic" since these qualities can lead to an undermining of the bureaucratic culture upon which modern administrative techniques are established. Traditionally, such requirements have been reflected in the British educational system, with those graduating from the "elite" universities being selected for future senior management positions in which, in the exercise of their own creativity, responsibility and discretion, they manage others. These people, in turn, through their own schooling and university experiences, can be relied upon to undertake their organizational tasks in a compliant, routine and bureaucratic fashion (Brown and Lauder 1992).

It is for these reasons that British companies continue to be characterized by a particular feature, namely, the selection of future senior managers from a very restricted number of elite universities (Handy 1987). For such positions, the experiences of elite forms of higher education that encourage the exercise of "independent thought" and "judgement" are seen as essential. For middle and junior managerial positions on the other hand, there is a tendency to recruit from the less prestigious schools, colleges and Institutions of Higher Education (IHEs) which recruit those who have enjoyed a particular pattern of family and childhood socialization. Hence, they are inclined to select middle-class white males (and increasingly females) who are perceived to be capable of ultimately filling "middle" management positions. It is assumed that these students possess the necessary personal characteristics to perform their duties in a compliant and routinized manner. The growth of large-scale organizations, then, structured on the basis of Fordist or bureaucratic principles, have had a number of implications for the nature of class relationships, social mobility and for the rôle of IHEs in Britain (Perkin 1989). Certainly, during the early postwar decades, the structuring of organizations according to bureaucratic principles offered relatively secure middle-class career paths (Wilensky 1962).[2] By undertaking their work tasks according to clearly-specified procedures and precisely-formulated job descriptions, they were able to enjoy reasonably high earnings and social status. As middle managers, they commanded "respect", both within the workplace and in the wider community (Pahl and Pahl 1971). Accordingly, the expansion of the middle class, claimed to be symptomatic of the affluence of the 1960s and early 1970s, was contingent upon the development of organizational forms that required the recruitment of people for the rapidly expanding number of "routine" corporate managerial positions (Young and Willmott 1973). A consequence of these organizational processes was the perception of a class structure that was breaking down because of fluid and growing occupational opportunities.

However, since the early 1970s the bureaucratic paradigm that has shaped the modern corporation and notions of managerial competence has been subject to revision and reform. A number of factors contributed to this change in mood among corporate managers, three of which seem to be particularly pertinent. First, the oil crisis of 1973 not only increased the production costs of British companies, but also weakened the competitive position of the British economy as a whole. Secondly, this sense of economic decline was fuelled by the rapid industrialization of Pacific Rim countries and an apparent ability to outperform British companies in an increasingly competitive global economy. Therefore, the competitive success of Japanese and Pacific Rim companies was forcing many corporate leaders to review their business practices and to reassess the cost-effectiveness of Fordist and bureaucratic-based management systems (Harvey 1989). Thirdly, the early 1970s witnessed a series of industrial disputes which led to the development of a widespread opinion among corporate leaders that management had lost the will, competence and/or right to manage, and that organized labour had become the dominant economic and political force. Within a corporatist framework of industrial relations it was commonly argued that excessive wage demands from organized labour had led to an accelerated fall in profit margins. As a result, corporate bosses claimed that they were reluctant to invest in new productive capacity and to expand their business operations in Britain.

Cost effective pressures have also become increasingly evident within public sector organizations, such as in the remaining state owned utilities, health, welfare and education institutions. With the election of the 1979 Conservative government, committed to reducing the public sector borrowing requirement, lowering overall levels of personal taxation, and "cutting back" the rôle of the state in the economy as a whole, public sector managers were under similar pressures to review their costs and to reappraise the effectiveness of their organizational and management practices. These trends continue today as private and public sector organizations strive to be more cost effective and efficient. Managers, accordingly, are pressurized constantly to achieve higher levels of measurable performance. Demands for greater efficiency in uncertain market (and political) conditions mean that they can no longer be assured of relatively secure jobs with reasonably predictable career paths. In common with other categories of employees, they are now the victims of corporate restructuring such that their jobs and duties are frequently redesigned, changed and often made redundant (Handy 1989). Even those organizations that have expanded their trading activities over the past decade have often been able to do so without increasing managerial and other staff levels. Changes in national and global markets have led corporations to implement strategies geared to the production and sales of products and services for specialist "niches" rather than for general markets. Often, organizational restructuring has led to the setting-up of smaller, wholly owned subsidiaries and "strategic business units". Further, corporate strategies since the late 1970s are more likely to be concerned with achieving profits through consolidating and contracting trading activities rather than through generating high-volume growth. At the same time, the implementation of computer-based information systems has enabled senior management to cut overheads by reducing their need for routine clerical workers and various categories of junior and middle managers (Zuboff 1989). But perhaps most important of all, the economic and political pressures that have increasingly impinged upon the operation of large-scale organizations in both public and private sectors has brought about the demise of the bureaucratic paradigm, as the basis upon which effective and rational managerial decision-making can be structured. It has been superseded by "flatter", "looser" postbureaucratic organizational models which emphasize alternative attributes (Minzberg 1983).

A major part of the rhetoric within present-day senior management strategies is to abolish bureaucratic forms of organization, in order to eliminate cultures which foster risk avoidance and conformist, "ritualistic" forms of behaviour. The popularity of bureaucracy rested upon the extent to which operating procedures – characterized by the clear delineation of work tasks and responsibilities – sustained reliable, predictable, and compliant forms of behaviour. It was assumed that organizational goals could be achieved in a pre-planned and orderly fashion and with a minimum amount of ambiguity. However, in the 1990s there is an increasing recognition of the costs associated with these structures in their tendencies to mould "bureaucratic personality types" among employees who then prefer to value rôle conformity and job security rather than innovation and change. As a result, senior managers – particularly those within private-sector organizations – are anxious to encourage more "entrepreneurial" and "creative" forms of conduct among their middle-level and junior colleagues. Indeed, *intrapreneurship* is frequently used rhetorically to describe the attitudes of those managers who, working within "looser", less clearly defined organizational structures, adopt many of the attitudes and behaviours supposedly characteristic of "classical" 19th-century entrepreneurs (Minkes 1987).

There is, then, the growing popularity of organizational paradigms based upon principles and assumptions that are in sharp contrast to those underlying more bureaucratic forms. Instead of an emphasis upon clearly defined tasks, work rôles are broadly determined according to their contribution to the accomplishment of specific objectives. According to such paradigms, channels of communication are encouraged to be "open", "flexible" and "informal" rather than, as in bureaucratic structures, according to strictly prescribed rôles of authority. If reliability and conformity are valued attributes within bureaucratic management systems, in more loosely structured organizations a greater emphasis is supposed to be placed upon individual creativity and the capacity to cope with ambiguity and change. Managers are expected to be psychologically immersed in their jobs – rather than to rôle play as in bureaucracies – and it is for this reason that so much importance is attached to fostering appropriate organizational *cultures*, since it is through these rather than through explicitly stated rules and regulations that psychological involvement is to be obtained (Hofstede 1991).

It is ideals of this sort which are to be found in much of the rhetoric and many of the present-day panaceas advocated by management "gurus" as prescriptions for improving organizational effectiveness. Indeed, these seem to be growing in popularity among senior managers in both private and public-sector organizations as witnessed, for instance, in the worldwide success of Peters' and Watermans *In search of excellence* (1982). In this book, the authors argue that high-performing organizations have been able to reduce their dependency upon formalized structures and to implement cultures which encourage, among other things, "a basis for action", "autonomy and entrepreneurship", "productivity through people", "hands on, value driven leadership", and "simultaneous loose–tight" organizational properties. Similarly, other advocates of organizational change stress the desirability of "simple structures", "adhocracies" and "matrices" (Minzberg 1983). Hence it is argued that small and medium-sized companies enjoy considerable competitive advantages over larger organizations because their chief executives, who are often owner-managers, are able to exercise "direct" day-to-day control over their employees by cultivating open and informal systems of communication (Scase and Goffee 1989). Similarly, in large-scale organizations, it is claimed that the nurturing of "matrices" and "adhocracies", typically involving the utilization of ever-changing project teams and task forces, offer a means of overcoming more rigid departmental, functional or divisional boundaries in order to achieve particular goals. Further, for many large-scale organizations, the need for greater responsiveness to more competitive and rapidly changing market circumstances is expressed in the adoption of more "devolved" and "decentralized" structures. Hence the setting-up of "strategic business units" and shifts towards highly autonomous divisions, to which budgeting control and strategic management are delegated, represent attempts to be more responsive to the changing needs of different product markets. Some large corporations have even gone so far as to abandon altogether their divisionalized structures and to substitute in their place wholly owned subsidiary companies. The latter can enjoy almost total strategic and operational autonomy so long as they achieve a satisfactory level of performance as determined by their parent holding companies (Peters 1992).

Senior managers' rhetorical rejection of the bureaucratic paradigm has led to the implementation of a variety of organizational forms, many of which are subsumed under the general label of the "flexible" or "adaptive" firm (Atkinson 1985, Kanter 1989). Indeed, the extreme of this development is the organization which consists of little more than a small number of negotiators who agree trade terms with a variety of production subcontractors, who then sell on the products to wholesalers and retailers with no direct involvement in the production process itself. In such instances, the office and the telephone supersede the workplace and such organizations are little more than brokers in various products and services, negotiating trading terms with a broad range of subcontracting manufacturers, franchisees and others. If such forms of organization represent the "adaptive" firm in the extreme and hence only a very small number of organizations, their numbers are nevertheless increasing (Handy 1989). They are, for instance, growing rapidly in the media industry, where production processes in television and film, once undertaken in an integrated manner "in-house", are now fragmented and subdivided among a variety of "independent", self-employed "freelances" who are temporarily co-ordinated into "one-off" teams for the purposes of particular projects. As soon as a particular project is completed, the teams are dismantled and each freelance worker seeks engagement on another task with other groups of specialists.

If adaptive forms of organization are becoming a more pronounced feature of modern economic life, they are also reinforced by senior managerial attempts to change the nature of their corporate cultures. Just as organizations vary in their structural characteristics, they also differ in their predominant values and assumptions (Schein 1985). Highly bureaucratized organizations tend to foster cultures which emphasize the desirability of clearly defined rules and procedures for attaining operating efficiency. These encourage the adoption of routinized behaviour and reinforce a general psychological resistance to change. Established procedures will be assumed to be both effective and efficient and as such, not be regarded as cumbersome "red tape". Such *rôle cultures* tend to sustain values which give priority to "security" and "promotion" as rewards for staff who perform their duties satisfactorily, with loyalty and compliance (Handy 1985). Within bureaucratically structured organizations, therefore, predominant structures and cultures tend to be mutually reinforcing, so that employees come to exhibit "bureaucratic personalities". Hence, they develop cognitive styles which reduce their propensity to risk. It is in response to this that, alongside the introduction of more "adaptive" or "flexible" forms of organization, senior managers are drawing upon cultural paradigms which emphasize the value of experimentation, innovation, and creativity. They are attempting to foster values which stress goal achievement rather than rigid adherence to routines and procedures. Informal and intensive patterns of consultation and communication among colleagues is encouraged while, at the same time, vertical or hierarchical forms of managerial control – as exercised within traditional bureaucratic cultures – is underplayed.

Attempts to impose such changes have ramifications for management "style" and the ways in which senior managers control their staff. Within bureaucratic structures, senior managers can rely upon rules and formally-prescribed procedures, but in looser organizational forms there are fewer explicit guidelines that govern behaviour. In the relative absence of such rules and regulations, a greater emphasis is placed upon the use of a variety of interpersonal skills in order to motivate staff to achieve their goals (Scase and Goffee 1989). In the adaptive paradigm, these can be summed up by the use of the term *charismatic leadership* (see Chapter 2). Within newly evolving organizational forms, it is allegedly necessary for managers to work *with* their subordinates in order to achieve various specified goals. Instead of the imposition of orders and instructions through more traditional forms of "autocratic" management, it is stressed that managers need to develop leadership skills that encourage the sharing of problems and the discussion of possible solutions and strategies for achieving goals (Kanter 1989). The exercise of such skills presupposes that managers are flexible and accommodating in their attitudes, and that they adopt an *open-participative* approach to decision-making. This is particularly necessary within the context of project teams, where the successful attainment of goals is dependent upon personal compatibility, the sharing of ideas, and the commitment of highly-motivated staff. Further, the leadership skills stated to be required of managers within adaptive organizations focus upon their ability to understand and empathize with staff *as individuals* – in terms of understanding their personal job needs and motivation – and to be able to communicate with them on a close, intimate, and personal basis. Hence the psychological requirements of "competent" management within the newly emerging non-bureaucratic forms of organization are deemed to be more complex than those required in more traditional structures. If, within bureaucratic forms, managers could in the past manage through rules and procedures and thereby psychologically distance themselves from their staff, this is no longer the case. The adaptive organization demands a higher degree of psychological involvement in generating motivation and morale among staff, and, hence a greater understanding of human relations and interpersonal skills (Clegg 1990).

It is for these reasons that many corporate leaders are recognizing there is a problem of management development in Britain, because traditionally there has been over-dependence upon the bureaucratic form of organization with its need for "conformist" and "reliable" behaviour. With the development of more "flexible" or "adaptive" forms of organization, it is assumed that managers need to adopt more charismatic leadership skills. Hence, in the 1990s, corporate leaders are recognizing that the personal qualities previously associated with elite forms of higher education are now increasingly appropriate for a broader range of employees including middle managerial, technical specialist and those in skilled manual occupations.

Within IHEs this is reflected in the Enterprise in Higher Education Initiative (EHEI) which encourages universities to develop programmes for students to acquire the interpersonal – as well as technical – skills needed by more "adaptive" organizations. The Department of Employment's commitment to the ideals of an enterprise culture has led it to finance programmes in higher education that facilitate closer links between the universities and graduate employers (Jones 1990).[3] As a consequence, despite differences in emphasis among them, even the established universities are becoming more vocational in orientation, as is evident in the rapid expansion of business studies, law, accountancy, industrial psychology, economics and management courses and degrees.[4] This is leading to increasing conflicts between those who subscribe to traditional notions of a liberal education and those who are sympathetic to the more vocationally related rôle of the universities (Schuller 1991). However, within a newly emerging hierarchy of universities, it is the "lower status" universities that have sought to introduce personal and social skills training into the formal curriculum, along with more experimental forms of assessment (i.e. profiling), in response to the rhetoric of the new corporation. At the

11

same time the rhetoric of the adaptive organization has been used by graduate recruiters to make managerial careers more attractive to "established" university graduates by stressing the desirability of such personal attributes as "leadership", "creativity" and interpersonal skills. As such, the adaptive organization, in the importance that it attributes to informality, openness in patterns of consultation and communication, emphasises attributes not unlike those which graduates experience within their various university settings. Indeed, some organizations deliberately attempt to foster such similarities. In high technology companies such as those found in the electronics and pharmaceutical industries as well as in such areas as advertising, broadcasting, publishing and the popular media, management often goes to great lengths to "recreate" the cultures of the established universities (Peters and Waterman 1982). Work is defined as a sphere for self-fulfilment, and a high value is attached to informality in dress, speech and patterns of interpersonal relations. Through these means, senior managers are attempting to recruit and retain high quality graduates who, over time, will acquire the necessary skills for charismatic leadership.

Although in Britain there is a major paradigm shift towards the adoption of more "adaptive" and "flexible" forms of organization, the extent to which this will be implemented in practice remains an open question. Moreover, how far this will result in a widespread exercise of charismatic leadership, drawing upon the innovative talents of larger numbers of employees, is uncertain. A major reason for this is to do with the nature of British culture, based as it is upon class divisions and "low trust" personal relationships which sustain traditional patterns of cultural reproduction (Fox 1974). In such circumstances the demonstration of senior management potential has depended upon elite conceptions of conduct in terms of interests, speech, dress, and personal appearance. It is further assumed that corporate "leaders" subscribe to values, attitudes and beliefs that could only be acquired through class-based family and educational experiences which, as a consequence, served to exclude low socio-economic groups, women and ethnic minorities. It is a style of leadership that fosters, and is dependent upon, "paternalistic" organizational cultures, so that women and those of ethnic and working-class origins are "disadvantaged" irrespective of their personal creativity, skills, competence or commitment to organizational goals. Therefore, without a significant change in dominant, elite-based cultural values, the shift towards adaptive forms of organization in the vast majority of corporations will be accompanied by efforts to maintain an emphasis on "moral authority", social distance and the enforcement of employee compliance through tighter surveillance, interpersonal competition and "stigma" for underperformance.

Likewise, although the rhetoric associated with the adaptive organization stresses the exercise of innovative and creative talent, the reality is likely to lead to attempts to recruit people, especially for the "fast-track" training programmes leading to senior managerial positions, who can be "trusted" to conform to the cultures of senior management and who are "acceptable" to both potential work colleagues and clients.

Hence the need to examine precisely how organizations are restructuring has become an urgent research question. Its importance is heightened by the fact that it has profound implications for the future rôle and organization of higher education. The expansion in student numbers and the rhetoric of personal and transferable skills which has informed recent debates about university curricula are premised on a fundamental change in the assumptions about the exploitation of human talent in corporate organizations (Kanter 1991). This, then, raises issues about the reproduction of cultural capital and the extent to which a shift in organizational paradigms will have real operational consequences for the recruitment and promotion of those who are likely to become senior managers. This, in turn, has implications for broader patterns of elite mobility and the rôle of IHEs in shaping personal opportunities as these come to reflect the changing "needs" of modern corporations. We turn our attention to these matters in the next chapter.

Notes

1. For the purposes of this book we adopt the notion of *paradigm* to refer to "ideal types" of organizational structure. As far as organizational change is concerned, corporate leaders often have implicit rather than explicit notions of preferred end-states and the term "adaptive" is often used as shorthand for describing the abandonment of bureaucratic forms of organization and the adoption of alternative structures and processes. Therefore, in management discussions these terms are often used in a "loose" rhetorical manner, a practice which is reinforced by a lack of detailed research into the relevant processes of change. For a discussion

of the problems associated with the use of "paradigms" in organization analysis, see Ackroyd 1992.

2. We define the "middle class" as those engaged in managerial, professional and specialist occupations while "working-class" is used to refer to those in routine non-manual and various categories of manual occupations (see Scase 1992).

3. The Enterprise in Higher Education Initiative was launched in 1987 with the intention of getting most of the larger Institutions of Higher Education (IHEs) involved by 1990. Jones (1990) writes:

> EHE is, in very general terms, a kind of TVEI for higher education. Many of the same ingredients are there – partnerships with employers, work-related curricula, work experience for students and staff, enterprising teaching and learning styles, accreditation of personal effectiveness as well as academic achievement, etc. (p. 86).

See also Brown and Turbin (1989).

4. In this study the established universities refer to those institutions which received their Royal Charter before 1990. The New Universities are the former Polytechnics which became integrated into a unified university system in England and Wales in 1992.

CHAPTER TWO

Education, recruitment and changing patterns of cultural reproduction

An assumption which underpins most contemporary discussions about the efficiency and effectiveness of organizations is that they are heavily dependent upon the quality of human resources (McGregor 1960, Ginzberg 1966). The significance attached to education as a source of organizational efficiency results from the perceived need for more technical, professional, and managerial workers in an increasingly competitive global economy (Organisation for Economic Co-operation and Development [OECD] 1989; Confederation of British Industry [CBI] 1989). However, for the last twenty years the education system has been treated by conservative politicians and industrialists with increasing suspicion, as the promise of continuous economic growth and low unemployment has proved untenable since the early 1970s. Rather like the talented student who under-achieves due to "laziness", the education system at all levels has been subject to reprimand and reform (Jones 1989). Higher education has not escaped the critical gaze of New Right critics and has also been subject to a programme of "marketization" (see Chapter 3).

Criticism of the educational system has become a predictable response when corporate performance and economic conditions deteriorate. However, underlying assertions that education is failing to meet the needs of industry is an acknowledgement of more deep rooted changes in the nature of economic competition, technological innovation and organizational restructuring. Moreover, despite a reappraisal as to how education should be organized and funded, faith in the educational system to deliver the economic "goods" has not been questioned, and the idea of education as a form of investment rather than consumption has remained part of the conventional wisdom among politicians, employers, parents and students alike. The reassertion of this conventional wisdom – that national economic prosperity depends upon the quality of human resources – is reflected in the recent expansion of higher education (Ball 1990). It is also reflected in the buoyant demand for higher education, given an assessment that it offers the best route into senior positions within organizations.

We can identify two competing explanations of the relationship between education and occupational stratification – the *technocratic* theory and the *social exclusion* theory. The technocratic explanation conforms closely to conventional wisdom (Kerr et al. 1973, Bell 1973).

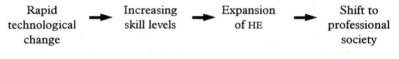

| Rapid technological change | → | Increasing skill levels | → | Expansion of HE | → | Shift to professional society |

The technocratic model

It is assumed that rapid technological change is an endemic feature of advanced industrial societies. Consequently, a much larger proportion of jobs require extensive periods of formal education and training, while the proportion of semi-skilled and unskilled jobs declines over time. Support for this view is found in the increasing importance of "human capital" as the dominant form of wealth in advanced capitalist societies (Schultz 1961, Vaizey 1962). From this perspective, the expansion of higher education during the second half of the 20th century can be explained in terms of the pressure placed upon governments to invest in higher education in order to ensure the supply of professional, managerial and technical workers required in a "hightech" society. In these terms, the labour market is characterized by a hierarchy of occupations which reflects a division of "skilled" labour, matched with a hierarchy of talent reflected in the competition for academic and professional credentials. Therefore the ideology of meritocracy which underpins the competition for access to higher education and better paid and more prestigious occupations is understood to reflect a political determination to equalize opportunities to ensure that talented members of society are able to realize their potential, irrespective of class, gender or race (Parsons 1959). This, it is argued, is because advanced industrial societies can no longer afford to squander talent among disadvantaged social groups if they are to remain economically efficient.

| Increasing competition between occupational/ social groups | → | Little change in skill levels/ deskilling | → | Expansion of HE reflects credential inflation | → | Middle class monopolization of superior jobs |

The social exclusion model

The theory of *social exclusion* questions technical function theory on both theoretical and empirical grounds (Collins 1977, 1979). [1] On theoretical grounds it is critical of accounts which assume that you can read off the structure, organization and content of higher education simply in terms of the "logic of industrialism" or the "needs of industry". On the contrary, it suggests that the ideologies, traditions and content of education systems are multifaceted, and that the power play of competing vested interest groups is vital to a full understanding of both educational change and the labour market. On empirical grounds, social exclusion theorists argue that there is little evidence to support the claim that skill levels have risen dramatically during the second half of the 20th century. Indeed, some have suggested that, on balance, late capitalism is characterized by a process of de-skilling rather than up-skilling or re-skilling (Braverman 1974, Bowles and Gintis 1976), and that there is also little evidence to support the assertion that college trained workers are more productive than those who have not had the benefit of higher education (Berg 1970). Collins (1979) also suggests that schools have little effect on learning, apart from the fact that they mould those "disciplined cultural styles already prominent among the higher social classes; grades simply reward and certify displays of middle-class discipline". This has led him to ask "how do we account for the fact that modern America has come to be stratified around an educational credential system with a stranglehold on occupational opportunities and a technocratic ideology that cannot stand close examination?" His answer is that social groups are concerned with finding ways of gaining and controlling occupational power and income. In such circumstances, educational credentials are used to provide the means of building specialized professional and technical enclaves, along with hierarchical staff divisions. Therefore the expansion of higher education represents a conflict between social groups for scarce credentials rather than a demand for more technically skilled workers. Moreover, the "conventional wisdom" serves an invaluable ideological function in legitimating the monopoly which professional groups command over entry requirements, and selection to their ranks. When standards of entry are raised in the name of the increasing complexity of professional occupational rôles, this reflects the exclusionary tactics of professional groups, seeking to limit the number of recruits. It therefore serves to legitimate the use of credentials as a way of screening students for different segments of the labour market, based upon social position and power rather than individual talent (Weber 1978, p. 1000). From this perspective, what is happening in both the educational system and the labour market is both unfair, and probably inefficient.

We concur with Collins that the technocratic view is flawed both theoretically and empirically. One only has to look at differences in international rates in post-compulsory education to recognize that they cannot be explained in technocratic terms (Chisholm 1992). But he overplays his hand. To assume that there has been no increase in the knowledge requirement of a larger proportion of jobs in the 1990s compared to the postwar decades would be incorrect. There are a number of studies in Western capitalist societies, albeit since the time Collins wrote *The credential society* (1979), which have shown that skill levels have been increasing (Block 1990), although this is certainly not true of all jobs (Brown and Scase 1991, Gallie 1991). Part of the weakness of Collins' argument is that he examines the technocratic account in its own terms, by attempting to assess the impact of technology on skill levels. Paradoxically, this has led him to obscure the fact that the introduction of new technologies is never simply a technical issue; it is dependent on, and presumes, an organizational context which can either enhance or repress the level of discretion and trust between management and workers (Fox 1974; Sabel 1982). In other words, the demand for more highly educated labour may reflect a change in managerial and organizational paradigms as much as that which has resulted from the rapid pace of technological innovation. Moreover, we need to make a distinction between actual skills used to undertake jobs and what employers think they need. The question then becomes "why do they perceive their needs in these terms?" To suggest that it simply reflects credential inflation ignores the possibility of significant changes in the nature of corporate organization and changes in employer conceptions of professional and managerial competence. However, the impact of organizational restructuring and changes in the system of higher education on occupational stratification and social class has (so far) received little attention.

To what extent is the growing significance of cultural capital (Bourdieu and Passeron 1977), albeit in an elaborated and hidden form, reinforcing social and educational inequalities and inhibiting the development of innovative and creative talents specifically among the expanding numbers of the higher educated? What, then, are the implications of the restructuring of corporate organizations for the structure, content, and competing demands made on IHEs? More specifically, what facets of "human" and "cultural" capital will be valued in adaptive organizations? Table 2.1 summarises some of the key features involved in the shift from bureaucratic to adaptive organizations. Although it presents the changes in terms of "ideal types", it highlights our contention that if these changes come to approximate empirical reality, it will necessitate both a change in our understanding of managerial qualities and in the relationship between education and the labour market for the more highly educated. If higher education does reward and certify the display of middle-class self-discipline, as Collins suggests, the dominant mode of disciplined cultural style among the middle classes is being recast in a way that will result in a growing contradiction between education and the labour market (Brown and Lauder 1992). Thus, it could be argued that it will make it increasingly difficult for working-class students to acquire the appropriate kinds of "cultural capital" for employment and occupational success in adaptive organizations, despite the rhetoric of cultural diversity rather than superiority. This change in cultural code can be summarized in terms of a shift from a *bureaucratic* to a *charismatic* personality, which is compatible with the paradigm shifts that are occurring in organization design.[2]

The assignment of tasks within bureaucratic organizations is based on technical qualifications and competences, assessed through formalized, impersonal procedures and examinations. Indeed, the bureaucratic personality is one which emphasizes a high degree of conformity and rule-following behaviour, and the reliable and routine

Table 2.1   Changing organizational paradigms.

	Bureaucratic	Adaptive
Selection	Individual attributes De-personalized	Personal qualities Personality package
Socialisation	Compartmentalized Inter-positional Rule following	Holistic Inter-personal Code cracking, rule making
Cognitive style	Bureaucratic personality	Charismatic personality
Symbolic/social control	Impersonal Explicit ground rules	Personalized Implicit ground rules
Promotion/success	Explicit achievement criteria based on bureaucratic work programme	Implicit achievement criteria based on inter-personal compatibility and performance
Corporate culture	Weak	Strong

performance of prescribed tasks based on explicit rules and rituals. In the same way that bureaucratic work involves extensive use of categorization and compartmentalization premised on the application of abstract rules, so there is a clear separation between the private social world of the individual and the public, "visible" rôle of the corporate official (Bernstein 1975). The preservation of personal space and intimate relationships divorced from the impersonal and public performance of bureaucratic routine is a dominant feature of the bureaucratic personality. Moreover,

> The bureaucrats official life is planned for him [or her] in terms of a graded career, through the organizational device of promotion by seniority, pensions, incremental salaries, etc., all of which are designed to provide incentives for disciplined action and conformity to the official regulations. The official is tacitly expected to and largely does adapt his [or her] thoughts, feelings and actions to the prospect of this career. (Merton 1949, 200–201)

In adaptive organizations, on the other hand, the bureaucratic personality is a source of "trained incapacity" as the forms of learning and socialization in bureaucratic organizations become an obstacle to successful performance in new organizational settings (see Merton 1964, 197–8). In other words, it is not only a situation where the goalposts have been moved, but where the rules of the game have also been changed.

According to the adaptive paradigm, managerial qualities can be described in terms of the "charismatic personality". The idea of the charismatic personality is one which values those who seek to break the structures of routine actions and rule-following, to replace them with patterns of innovative and creative behaviour. "The charismatic person is the creator of a new order as well as the breaker of routine order" (Shils 1965, 1968). They are also able to work or manage others collectively through the use of charismatic rather than bureaucratic authority. Max Weber's (1978) definition of charismatic leadership applies to a small number of "extraordinary" individuals such as among religious prophets, military heroes, or political leaders. Our use of the term follows Edward Shils' (1958) distinction between this form of "extraordinary" charisma based on intense and concentrated action, from what Shils views as its "normal" form, which is more attenuated and dispersed. In adaptive organizations there is a need for an infusion of charismatic leadership because of the need to see the "bigger picture" and to avoid what Kanter (1984) calls "segmental thinking". The emphasis is upon "can do" rather than "will do". In essence, the charismatic personality is the opposite of the bureaucratic in that it is based on personal and interpersonal skills. The ability to get on with others and to identify with a strong management-based corporate culture is paramount. This often means that the division between private life and working life, between the "official" and the "personal", is broken, leading to an exposure of the "whole" person in the assessment of adequate performance, rather than simply the outward measure of objective, impersonal rôle performance which characterized bureaucratic organizations.

However, it remains to be seen whether British companies will make a significant move from bureaucratic to adaptive organizational forms. The extent to which they will seek charismatic rather than bureaucratic qualities among their "core staff" will depend on the types of enterprise and the job tasks to be fulfilled. Even if the changes outlined in this book remain nascent, the implications for education and organizational socialization and selection are far-reaching. Indeed, it is plausible to argue that most of the complaints levelled at the educational system for failing to meet the needs of employing organizations over the past decade or more are not the result of the schools, colleges or universities doing anything different or less competently than in the past, but rather, at least in terms of demand for the more highly educated, they reflect a change in the perceived needs of the recruiters for more "flexible" and "adaptable" workers, with more developed interpersonal "social skills". As the definition of managerial qualities and modes of control shifts from the bureaucratic and impersonal to the charismatic and personalized, so the "rules of entry" and "rules of the game" incorporate more elements that are implicit and unknowable in advance. Unless job applicants share the same cultural understandings and disposition as the recruiter, they will find it difficult to "decode" the rules by which the selection process is being played. In other words, there is likely to be a change in "cultural code" that will make social background, gender and ethnic identities more exposed (visible) and significant for entry to managerial jobs and for career progression (Bernstein 1975). Paradoxically, as a consequence of employers emphasizing a need for flexible, innovative and creative talents and the interpersonal skills required for team work, *personal compatibility* with other group members becomes more important.

It is no longer enough to acquire the appropriate credentials and to show evidence of technical competence. It is now the *whole* person who is on show and at stake in the market for managerial and professional work. It is the "personality package" based on a combination of technical skills, credentials, and charismatic qualities which must be sold (Fromm 1962). We are not suggesting that social considerations have been eliminated in bureaucratic organizations. In Britain the elites were distinguished by and expected to exhibit a "cultural code" consistent with images of managerial authority, expert knowledge, self-control, rational behaviour, and decision-making. Halsey (1962) recognized, in a comparison with Britain and the United States:

> The English businessman will not look for a training in psychology or industrial sociology in his managerial recruits but rather for the vaguely defined qualities of the Oxbridge man. (p. 507)

Conversely, the importance of technical skills, alongside "personality", was recognized by Erich Fromm (1949):

> Even the best bedside manner and the most beautifully equipped office on Park Avenue would not make a New York doctor successful if he did not have a minimum of medical knowledge and skill. Even the most winning personality would not prevent a secretary from losing her job unless she could type reasonably fast. However, if we ask what the respective weight of skill and personality as a condition for success is, we find that only in exceptional cases is success predominantly the result of skill and of certain other human qualities like honesty, decency, and integrity. Although the proportion between skill and human qualities on the one hand, and "personality" on the other hand as prerequisites for success varies, the "personality factor" always plays a decisive rôle. Success depends largely on how well a person sells himself on the market, how well he gets his personality across, how nice a "package" he is; whether he is "cheerful", "sound", "aggressive" "reliable", "ambitious"; furthermore, what his family background is, what clubs he belongs to, and whether he knows the right people. (pp. 69–70)

What we are suggesting here is that the shift from bureaucratic to charismatic qualities among managerial and professional workers has placed an increasing importance on the "personality package" with respect to a much broader range of management jobs, and not simply to those located within the uppermost echelons of organizations.

Employers will nowadays translate their need for flexible, innovative and creative employees into concerns about how "personalities" fit into the changing interpersonal dynamics of the adaptive organization.[3] Paradoxically, or rather predictably in Britain, the increasing importance attached to group and team work becomes translated into the need for "safe bets", that is, people with the appropriate cultural capital who will understand the "invisible" cultural code that has replaced the "visible" bureaucracy. In other words, it requires people it can "trust". This can put those of working-class origins, women and ethnic minorities at a distinct disadvantage within the adaptive organization. Although "impersonality", "objectivity" and other such "traits" are often seen to be "masculine" attributes and the shift towards interpersonal skills would appear to favour the expressive features of the "feminine", in adaptive organizations senior managers are less constrained by the formal and explicit criteria which regulate promotion processes as in bureaucratic organizations (Smith 1990). Hence women and other minority groups are likely to be disadvantaged within the opportunity structures of adaptive organizations which lead to senior managerial positions (Davidson and Cooper 1992). Therefore it may be suggested that as the qualities of charismatic leadership are seen to be more important, so the ability to work with other colleagues becomes paramount. In turn, there will be a tendency for those already in higher positions to reproduce the organization in their "own image", that is, middle-class, white and usually male.

On the basis of this argument, it can be claimed that even if there has been an increase in the demand for managerial, professional and technical employees, the expansion of higher education (HE), and the growing demand for academic credentials which this reflects, is in conflict with the nurturing of the assumed managerial qualities required in adaptive organizations.[4] Students and staff continue to adhere to bureaucratically inspired assumptions both in terms of the educational process and in sustaining occupational expectations. The formula for success is "compliance for knowledge, knowledge for qualifications, and qualifications for superior jobs". This "credential nexus" is perfect as a preparation for jobs requiring managers engaged in rule-following behaviour within bureaucratic organizations. Education by "followership" has given rise to a variety of *instrumental* attitudes and orientations which have led to the "cult of the grade" (Bourdieu and Passeron 1964). This focus on the grading of academic performance is, of course, eagerly reinforced by academic staff in order to win compliance and maintain the distinction between "winners" (staff) and "contestants" (students). But as recruiters more frequently express the need for charismatic rather than bureaucratic qualities in their recruits, the competition for credentials is inhibiting students' acquisition of personal and social skills. This is particularly noticeable among students from working-class and lower-middle-class backgrounds, who are primarily concerned to pull themselves, with every essay and examination mark, away from their social roots, because they have neither the social confidence – gained in the security of the middle-class cultural code(s) – nor the "escape routes" that give students, especially of the old middle classes, more access to material as well as cultural capital.[5]

24

Whereas qualifications used to provide employers with a reasonably good predictor of occupational competence, they are less likely to do so today because of the changing nature of professional and managerial work. In large scale bureaucratic organizations, qualifications were a better predictor because there was a close relationship between education and work experiences. The possession of a graduate qualification provided evidence of the bureaucratic discipline and competence demanded for managerial positions in both private and public sector organizations – disciplined study involved in mastering a body of knowledge; meeting examination deadlines; compliance with authority, etc. Yet if organizations adhere to paradigms which emphasize creative, innovative, habit breaking rather than habit making behaviour, so credentials become an increasingly inadequate basis for recruitment into a broader range of jobs. However, the education system continues to place an overriding emphasis on objective academic performance, although there has been some attempt at "profiling" in less prestigious institutions in order to assess a range of student qualities which extend beyond purely academic performance.[6] The problem with extending non-academic qualities is that the basis for assessment becomes necessarily more subjective and holds little sway on the academic market, where degrees of worth are judged exclusively in terms of academic criteria. Moreover, as we will show in a later chapter, despite increasing demands from employers for educational institutions to develop a broader range of personal and social skills that are underdeveloped and undervalued in most universities, when employers are recruiting for their fast-track graduate development programmes they continue to target students in the established universities. This is despite the far greater willingness of the "new" universities to develop curricula and forms of assessment which seek to satisfy employer demands for "rounded" rather than academically narrow recruits.

There is also a further contradiction between a commitment to the "credential nexus" and student expectations that this will provide access to occupational careers, which has significant implications for our understanding of education and occupational stratification. Whereas the social elite have continued to enjoy the benefits of private education throughout the 20th century, the demand that they equip their incumbents with academic credentials has increased. The changing demand for academic credentials among the middle class as a whole has been noted by Bourdieu and Boltanski (1978), who argue that the increasing demand for education is closely linked to broader changes in social structure, especially the bureaucratization of recruitment practices used by large corporations and professional organizations. This has resulted in the growing demand for certification among the middle class in order to reproduce their social advantage, as well as from the working-class as an avenue of upward mobility. The increasing instrumentalism among middle-class pupils and students has been a response to economic recession, high rates of unemployment and a recognition that degree level study is vital to gain access to professional and managerial work. The acquisition of educational credentials has become an even more important insurance policy, minimizing the likelihood of unemployment and downward social mobility. Those who have monopolized university education in the past – white, middle class males – confront increasing competition for university places from female students from similar backgrounds. Moreover, access to educational credentials remains the key to working-class social mobility, especially at a time when large numbers of traditional working-class jobs have disappeared.

However, a consequence of economic restructuring has been to undermine traditional patterns of career progression within public and private sector organizations. Career advance through internal labour markets has become an increasingly risky strategy, especially in private companies, given the increasing propensity for corporations to be taken-over, broken-up, or rationalized. The consequences for employees are frequently enforced career moves, redundancy, or early retirement. The acquisition of externally validated qualifications is being used increasingly as a way of insulating managers and company executives against the vagaries of the global market and corporate restructuring (Brown 1990). This trend not only helps us to explain the increasing demand for business studies at both undergraduate and postgraduate levels – for instance, the massive expansion of MBA full and part-time programmes – but also the increasingly instrumental attitudes of middle class parents concerning the education of their children. The populist appeal of the enterprise culture and personal improvement through the acquisition of material property is correctly understood by the middle classes to be a risky business (Coffield and MacDonald 1991). Social status and security are more reliably secured through the acquisition of cultural capital (especially academic qualifications from prestigious institutions), which facilitates entry into professional and managerial employment. Despite employers expressing more concern about employees who are flexible, innovative and creative, there continues to be an inexorable shift towards all forms of technical, professional and managerial jobs requiring a graduate entry qualification. A degree has become the standard screening device for managerial and professional training. It is the key that unlocks (but does not necessarily open) doors. Hence, the competition for credentials has intensified as a larger proportion of labour market entrants have graduate qualifications. In this case education becomes

a defensive necessity to private individuals even if there are no net social returns to education . . . Education becomes a good investment, not because it would raise an individual's income above what it would have been if no one had increased their education, but because it raises their income above what it will be if others acquire an education and they do not. (Thurow and Lucas, in Hirsch 1977, 51).

Moreover, given an increasing polarization within the graduate labour market between the fast-track training programmes leading to senior managerial positions and those junior or middle managerial positions which offer little opportunity for career advancement (to say nothing of the large numbers of graduates who are unemployed or forced into contingent work – as part-time waiters, teachers of English to foreign students during the summer months or temporary shelf-fillers in supermarkets – these factors have all combined to intensify middle-class efforts to ensure that their children acquire the appropriate form of "cultural capital". As Alfred Marshall (1920) recognized, "The professional classes especially, while generally eager to save some capital *for* their children, are even more alert for opportunities of investing it *in* them" (p. 562).

What this discussion suggests is that even if there has been an increase in the proportion of jobs requiring a significant skills base, changes in the education system and labour market are heightening the importance of cultural capital in the "competition for a livelihood" (Weber 1978, 341). Given that few middle-class families can maintain their social position through direct inheritance, or through monopolistic control over the market for superior jobs, the key to occupational success is through access to market power – that is, resources in the market place – rather than influence over markets (Hirsch 1977, 153). Within classical economics, "capital" is defined in material terms such as equipment, materials, goods and labour costs. A more complete concept of capital, which includes "human" capital, was outlined in Irving Fisher's *The nature of capital and income* (1927) and marked the beginning of attempts to measure the economic returns of investments in education and training. Fisher's definition of capital treats "all sources of income streams as forms of capital" (see Schultz 1968). In this sense it is not only possible to talk about "codified" and "certified" knowledge and skills as a potential source of capital, but also as "cultural" capital (Bourdieu and Passeron 1977).[7] Not everyone has access to the same cultural resources, in the sense of cultural identities based on different patterns of socialization, language codes, and cultural artefacts. The cultural disposition of a child or student, for instance, can be capitalized in the school in terms of the harmony (or lack of it) between what is taught, modes of transmission, and motivation to learn school knowledge as a result of parental, teacher or peer group pressures. Cultural capitalization in school takes the form of access to qualifications which can ultimately be traded in the labour market for jobs offering high status and income. In this sense, the cultural resources/disposition of a child can contribute to or inhibit educational and later economic success. This is not to suggest that those with the "wrong" cultural background cannot achieve within education or labour market institutions: there are many examples of children from working-class or ethnic minority backgrounds who are "sponsored" through the system and acquire the appropriate forms of cultural capital on the way.[8]

Moreover, whereas technocratic theory treats the acquisition of expert knowledge and formal skills in a neutral way – a product of a meritocratic race, which creates a hierarchy of skills, matched with the technical requirements of employers, cultural capital emphasizes the fact that these processes do not take place in a social vacuum. They are dependent upon social differences in access and responses to education, and employer definitions of the kinds of employees they are seeking. These are never based purely on the technical competence of the individual jobseeker. We know that even with similar qualifications and work experience, a black job seeker is less likely to get a job than a white person (Ward and Cross 1991). Men, even if trained in child care, will find it more difficult to get a job as a child minder because of the gendered demarcations of many jobs (Walby 1986). Moreover, the evaluation of cultural capital is contingent upon the supply of particular kinds of workers, and the demand for the skills, knowledge or attributes they are seen to possess. It is this dominant code of cultural capital which is changing, so that "individual attributes" are now reinforced by notions of "personal qualities". What we want to argue here is that cultural capital has not only come to assume increasing importance in the distributive struggle for managerial and professional occupations, but has also been associated with a change in its form. The acquisition of cultural capital based upon individual attributes such as education, credentials, gender, and ethnicity, has been extended to incorporate explicitly those "personal qualities" that expose the "inner world" of human personality, motivation and interpersonal compatibility. In other words, to be successful in the competition for managerial and professional occupations, good academic credentials have to be presented as part of a package of experience, achievement, social skills, and human personality.

The social significance of this change in the nature of cultural capital is due to the fact that these personal qualities are not only acquired in an indirect way through the acquisition of scarce academic and professional credentials, but also as a direct consequence of patterns of middle-class socialization and life-styles, where the cultivation of interests and investment in leisure, hobby pursuits, and patterns of personal interaction serve to embellish a "privileged" education. Therefore, the selection to elite schools, universities, and superior jobs has become more overtly "social", involving an exhibition of those personal qualities which symbolize "safe bets". Although property relations have always been related to the acquisition of cultural capital (Bourdieu and Passeron 1977), the reinforcement of individual attributes with personal qualities as the dominant form of cultural capital heightens the importance of having sufficient disposable income to pay for educational fees and other socially acceptable lifestyle activities.

Thus, in order to understand the full impact of the changes in work organization and recruitment to managerial and professional jobs, the rôle of higher education assumes considerable significance. In recent years the government has tried to reform higher education in order to conform to the stated needs of employers (Her Majesty's Stationery

Office (HMSO) 1990). As a result there has been a phase of rapid expansion in student numbers, attempts to increase the vocational relevance of university courses, and the creation of a "single" market within which universities must compete for students and research funds (Department of Education and Science (DES) 1991, Hague 1991, Finegold et al. 1992). Therefore, in light of the above discussion we need to examine whether increasing access to higher education will lead to greater educational and occupational opportunities for non-traditional students; the ways in which cultural capital is nurtured and deployed by different student groups; and how students orientate themselves to the labour market. Prior to an empirical investigation of these questions, we attempt to locate recent reforms in higher education within an historical context. What this initial discussion highlights is a long standing "creative tension" between pressures on higher education to generate an adequate supply of "knowledgeable" workers, and the attempt by the middle classes to monopolize social and educational opportunities for their children. Although the gloss on the expansion of higher education emphasizes equal opportunities and democratization, the increasing importance attached by employers to the *direct* value of middle-class forms of cultural capital, cloaked in the jargon of personal and transferable skills, will ensure that some graduates are more equal than others. The regulation of talent within higher education is the subject of the next chapter.

Notes

1. In this discussion we will focus on the work of Randall Collins because he explicitly addresses the issues which are central to this book. The "social exclusion" model of social and occupational stratification derives from the writings of Max Weber (1978), and has been developed by a number of other writers, including Parkin 1979, Murphy 1988, and Witz 1992.

2. The conceptual thinking that underpins this discussion is greatly indebted to the work of Basil Bernstein (1975) and Eric Fromm (1949).

3. If the emphasis is on corporate cultures and group work, then there is less room for mavericks. This is likely to reinforce the use of credentials and selection on the basis of the appropriate cultural capital. Collins argued that educational credentials were most heavily emphasized within organizations stressing normative control (cultural socialization), especially in

large bureaucratic organizations (Collins 1979, 48). Recent changes in organizational structures are likely to reinforce and extend this practice.

4. This applies equally to much of the contemporary debate about the educational system's failure to meet the needs of employing organizations.

5. Although this is a poor second best for those who have recently acquired wealth and who are keen to translate some of their material capital into cultural capital in the form of their children.

6. The legitimation function of the education system will make it very difficult for schools, colleges and universities to shift from its formal/objective mode of selection and assessment to a more subjective basis of selection, because of its need to maintain its "meritocratic" and "rational" character.

7. Of course, human knowledge, skills, or cultural attributes remain potential sources of capital unless they are utilized in the market for labour, information, etc., in the same way that Karl Marx made the distinction between labour power (the potential to labour) and labour (actual work conducted).

8. We would also distance ourselves from Bourdieu in that he has tended to define cultural capital in spatial terms – the space between working-class and middle-class dispositions which put the former at a distinct advantage in schools because it is more in tune with middle-class cultural values. This leads Bourdieu towards a passive view of human action (Jenkins 1992), and working-class responses are understood in terms of their "inability to respond" to the demands of the "middle-class" school (Brown 1987).

CHAPTER THREE

Higher education and
the regulation of talent

In advanced industrial nations the managerial, professional and technical elites are increasingly composed of people with higher education, despite important national differences. In the USA and Japan some 85 per cent of senior managers have degrees, while the figure for Britain is 24 per cent (Handy 1989, 123). This reflects distinct ideologies, traditions, and educational policies in different societies, as well as differences in the use of academic qualifications in occupational selection (Anderson 1962, Green 1990). In England in the 19th century, higher education was solely vocational, developed on the European university self-governing model from the monastic disciplines, for training the priesthood and later embracing the professions of law and medicine. Following political and industrial revolutions, the landed aristocracy preserved its position in society by cultivating an elite culture based upon Greek and Latin classics. The generally accepted version of events is that the rising industrial and commercial elites with whom it shared power could buy land but could not buy social acceptance save by educating their sons to forsake trade and marry into the aristocracy, thus saving that social anachronism from extinction (Barnett 1986, Landes 1969). A practice which led the historian, Hugh Trevor-Roper, to comment that during the 19th century:

> an industrial revolution, having triumphed at home, was carried over the whole world by the elite of a society bred upon the literature of a city state and an empire whose slave-owning ruling class regarded industry and commerce as essentially vulgar.[1]

Nevertheless, although Oxford and Cambridge Universities were imbued with the values of classical education, they continued to dominate recruitment to the established professions and into the upper echelons of the Civil Service. As Lowe (1990) has observed:

> By the start of the 20th century, it was virtually impossible to aspire to a senior position in the church, the public schools, the civil service or the law without having first been at Oxbridge (p. 12).[2]

Moreover, despite the fact that Britain was the first industrial nation, the expansion of higher education in the 19th century was not only a result of a growing demand for qualified scientists, technicians and inventors, but also because of the needs of members of the professions – in medicine, the civil service, and the legal system – to preserve or improve the social standing of their children. This growing demand was recognized by the Taunton Commission in 1868:

> The great majority of professional men, especially the clergy, medical men, and lawyers; the poorer gentry; all, in fact, who have received a cultivated education themselves . . . They have nothing to look to but education to keep their sons on a high social level. And they would not wish to have what might be more readily converted into money, if in any degree it tended to let their children sink in the social scale. The main evil of the present system, in their eyes, is its expense. (reprinted in Maclure 1968, 93)

Hence the relationship between the university and the economy for the middle classes centred on the preservation of social class and patriarchal relations as much as a concern to meet the increased need for formally trained employees which resulted from the introduction of industrial technologies and the exponential growth in scientific knowledge.[3] The established professions used higher education as a way of excluding social climbers from poorer social backgrounds by their exclusion from secondary and higher education, and by resisting claims to professional status from other occupational groups who sought to enhance their social standing by establishing their own professional examinations as with, for example, accounting and civil engineering (Collins 1979).[4] Moreover, given that higher education is a "specialized agency charged with the conservation of the most highly prized beliefs and intellectual skills in the cultural heritage" (Halsey 1962, 456), and that this cultural heritage was defined by the academic and social elites in terms of the education of the "gentleman", the vocational relevance of university education has historically been played down. It has taken much longer for the areas of technical and applied scientific and engineering studies to be accepted as suitable studies for institutions of higher learning, given the "legacy of Oxbridge domination, jealously guarding its seats of learning at the apex of the academic hierarchy, mirroring the power and prestige of the wider society" (Halsey 1962, 463, 1992a).[5] It is for these reasons Wiener (1981) blames the Oxbridge colleges for contributing to the decline of the industrial spirit in England.[6]

The development of the scientific and technical training required for the continued growth of industry was undertaken by the Victorian civic foundations in the commercial and industrial centres of London and the North of England. An attempt was made to emulate foreign industrial competitors, for example, the German university model was influential in establishing single science disciplines based upon research. As Sanderson (1972) has pointed out:

> From the civic universities industry demanded scientists and technologists, men with specific skills that could be directly applied to production or research.

However, even in the older science and technology-based civic universities there was a steady depreciation of vocational training in favour of the Victorian cult of gentlemanly amateurism.[7] This clearly represents an example of "academic drift", where lower status educational institutions attempt to enhance their reputations through the development of courses and curricula that emulate the elite universities. Moreover, with the growth of managerial and professional occupations, there was an increasing demand for higher education which reflected rising parental aspirations for their children. The fact that this was defined in terms of a liberal academic education rather than a vocational training was reinforced by the actions of employers who were keen to recruit Arts graduates for industrial as well as professional careers (Lowe 1990). As a result, the growth of the liberal professions was attended less by the educational transmission of occupational content and more by the communication of a culture and affinity with the capitalist and landed ruling class above them. This also served to maintain the social distance that separated managerial and professional groups from the manual working-class.

Before the Second World War, the elite English system of medieval Oxbridge colleges and Victorian civic universities were attended by only 3 per cent of the population – mainly young men – increasing to 7.2 per cent by 1962. Under pressure to expand due to further demands for technical and professional skills and an insatiable appetite for higher education among families of the "new" middle class, a phase of rapid growth was recommended in the 1963 Conservative-sponsored Robbins Report into higher education. The Report's recommendations led to the foundation of new universities and the promotion of a small number of polytechnics to independent university status. Robbins established the important principle that "courses of higher education should be available for all those who are qualified by ability and attainment to pursue them and who wish to do so". It thus guaranteed free higher education to those who qualified for it but, while ostensibly extending equality of opportunity, the Robbins principle did so on the basis of meritocratic selection. This was being phased out of the state school system by the introduction of comprehensive schools open to pupils of all abilities in place of selective grammar schools. Thus, selection was effectively moved up the age range.

The acceptance of the Robbins principle by the succeeding 1964 Labour government generated a pattern of transition for growing numbers of middle-class youth, female as well as male, moving from school to work and then to living away from home via three or four years' residential higher education. This "finishing school" model of HE was firmly established in what were largely liberal arts institutions patterned upon Oxford and Cambridge Universities. In postwar Britain most observers continued to emphasize the elitist nature of the established universities, enshrined in the ethos of the private schools and the Oxbridge image of the educated gentleman (Stanworth and Giddens 1974, Scott 1991). Indeed, the pattern of social mobility in Britain was characterized by Turner (1960) in terms of "sponsored" rather than "contest" mobility:

> *Contest* mobility is a system in which elite status is the prize in an open contest and is taken by the aspirants' own efforts. While the "contest" is governed by some rules of fair play, the contestants have wide latitude in the strategies they may employ. Since the "prize" of successful upward mobility is not in the hands of the established elite to give out, the latter are not in a position to determine who

shall attain it and who shall not. Under *sponsored* mobility, elite recruits are chosen by the established elite or their agents, and elite status is *given* on the basis of some criterion of supposed merit and cannot be *taken* by any amount of effort or strategy. Upward mobility is like entry into a private club, where each candidate must be "sponsored" by one or more of the members. Ultimately, the members grant or deny upward mobility on the basis of whether they judge the candidate to have the qualities that they wish to see in fellow members. (p. 856)

Even though the limited expansion of HE following Robbins was partly justified on the grounds of extending equality of opportunity, it hardly shifted the proportions of university students from manual and non-manual families, although it accommodated more working-class students in absolute numbers. Smithers and Robinson have estimated that the proportion of university entrants from managerial and professional backgrounds increased, from 62 per cent to 70 per cent, while those from manual workin-class backgrounds declined in the 1970s and 1980s.[8]

Alongside the expansion of the university system in the 1960s was investment in more vocationally orientated polytechnics and technical colleges, which were under the control of local education authorities. The expansion of the polytechnics was shaped by ideas that were in contrast to the traditions of the established universities. The aim of the polytechnics was to offer a "liberal vocationalism" (Silver and Brennan 1988) where course content more directly reflected the occupational destinations of students. Instruction tended to be programmatic, vocational and applied. They also aspired to become "the people's universities" (Robinson 1968), pioneering various forms of higher education for a "non-traditional" student population. Together with distance learning through the Open University (founded in 1969), the foundation and subsequent growth of the polytechnics brought the percentage of full- and part-time students in the United Kingdom to 12.7 per cent by the end of the 1970s. Nevertheless, social class divisions in access to higher education have continued despite recent demographic changes leading to a fall in the numbers of young people, and an absolute increase in student numbers. Between 1963 and 1990 the number of students increased from 216,000 to 1,086,300 with the participation rate moving from 7.2 per cent to 20.3

per cent (Halsey 1992b). However, Halsey, in the same publication, has also shown that the general tendency towards social class inequalities in higher education persists:

> For degree holders in 1974 whose fathers were professionals or managers, the ratio was 2.75, i. e. they were graduating at nearly 3 times the rate that would obtain if degree holding were randomly distributed. At the other extreme, the children of semi-skilled and unskilled workers had a ratio of 0.28 and the children of skilled manual workers 0.52. By 1985 these ratios had moved to 2.05, 0.36 and 0.50 respectively.

Whereas there has been little change in the proportion of undergraduates from manual working-class backgrounds, gender inequalities have narrowed (Statham et al. 1991). Before the Second World War less than a quarter of students in higher education were women, but by the end of the 1980s the proportion had increased to approximately 43 per cent. Female students have been particularly successful in gaining access to the erstwhile polytechnics where the number of full-time students in 1990 was almost identical to that of male students. In the established universities the number of full-time female students increased by 122 per cent between 1970 and 1990. The increase for male full-time students was 20 per cent.[9] What these changes reflect is the increasing number of women, especially from non-manual backgrounds, who are intent on pursuing full-time professional careers, and they often form relationships where both partners have to work in order to maintain an adequate standard of living (Crompton and Sanderson 1990). However, women remain as a small minority in the "hard" sciences: mathematics and economics (Thomas 1990). As a result, only 10 per cent of female graduates found scientific and engineering-related employment in 1989, compared to 32 per cent of males (DES 1991). Thus there is a forceful lobby for equal opportunities, challenging the tendency for certain courses, such as foreign languages, English literature and sociology to become "feminized".

Given the approximate 5.5 per cent average ethnic minority population of Britain – although higher for the younger generation, ethnic minority participation in higher education is already high: approximately 10 per cent of all admissions in 1990. The former polytechnics and college sector tend to admit more minority students than the established universities, as Evans has stated: "The polytechnics deal centrally with two aspects which are marginal in universities. One is race . . . the other aspect is age" (Evans 1993, 33; Brennan and McGeevor 1990). This figure also conceals sharp variations in participation rates of different ethnic groups as well as marked contrasts in their experiences of higher education. The pattern of ethnic minority participation is complex. An example is that more Indian males and Afro-Caribbean females achieve tertiary level qualifications than their white contemporaries (of the same gender) while Afro-Caribbean males and Bangladeshi and Pakistani students of both sexes represent the least qualified groups in the English education system (Department of Employment 1992). There are also differences in what ethnic students study, with Asians concentrated in accountancy, pharmacy and chemistry, and Afro-Caribbeans in the social sciences. Despite some blurring at the edges, this combination of class, gender, and race presents a familiar pattern in which the more "elite" institutions and courses continue to recruit a large proportion of middle-class, white males, despite a stated commitment to equal opportunities.

The development of higher education in England also needs to be set within a context of predominantly bureaucratic paradigms of work organization. The sharp distinction between "conception" and "execution" ensured that the proportion of employees requiring advanced academic or technical studies remained relatively small. Whereas in the United States, the extension of education until the age of 18 and having a college education became the norm for entry into technical, administrative and professional work, higher education in England remained the preserve of an elite. Therefore the relationship between education, recruitment and Fordist work practices in England not only ensured that higher education (especially in the university sector) was only available to a minority, but also had a profound impact on the form and content of educational experience. Indeed, the educational system has been premised on a set of rules, procedures and practices which conform to the principles of bureaucratic organization (Brown and Lauder 1992, 11). Within higher education, students have greater discretion over the use of their time. However, many aspects of bureaucratic education are in evidence, such as the lack of control students have over the content, pacing and grading of the learning process, the selection of textbooks, methods of assessment, and the management of the institution. Students quickly learn that there are certain hoops to jump through, such as the completion of assignments by a specified date, or the regurgitation of lecture notes in written examinations, which demand rule-following behaviour and an acceptance of the academic authority of teaching staff. There is little mileage to be gained from challenging the status quo, which leads to the label "disruptive" rather than "innovative" or "creative". Finally, the assessment of individual rather than collective work is sacrosanct. To work collectively in groups is to invite the charge of cheating rather than acceptance as a sign of mature interpersonal collaboration and co-operation (Brown and Lauder 1992). It is this apparent "mismatch" between education and the economy which has fuelled the latest period of expansion and reform. Employer fears about an inadequate supply of graduate labour to fill the increasing number of jobs demanding tertiary level education are reinforced by a political awareness that the competitive advantage currently enjoyed by Japan and the Pacific Rim countries is associated with a high proportion of employees with advanced academic qualifications (Confederation of British Industry (CBI) 1989).

However, with high rates of unemployment in Britain (Ashton 1991) denying literally millions of people the opportunity to develop any skills at work or to apply their education and experience in employment, the claim that a new "post-industrial" or "information society" has been created, demanding higher skills and greater theoretical knowledge from all its members sounds hollow, to say the least. The "official" justification for the expansion of higher education: that a modernized economy requires a workforce educated to the highest level possible, can be no more than an act of faith in an economic environment that has yet to deliver more than piecemeal technological modernization. Yet the policy of expansion is related to what Harvey calls "the uncomfortable transitions in many university systems in the advanced capitalist world from guardianship of knowledge and wisdom to ancillary production of knowledge for corporate capital" (Harvey 1989, 229). The policy justification for the government's newfound enthusiasm for expanding higher education is to be found, at least in part, in a switch from its policy of vocational training for the majority and academic education for a minority, based on an inadequately funded version of the German "dual system" of technical apprenticeship and academic schooling (Finn 1987) to an equally underfunded version of the North American mass system of higher education (Pearson and Pike 1989) as a way of dealing with the problem of permanent, structural youth unemployment (Ainley 1992).

However, in contrast to the succession of youth training schemes in the 1970s and 1980s, young people (and adults) have not had to be dragooned into higher education. This can be explained in part by the fact that in 1990 approximately 89 per cent of graduates were in employment, compared with just 62 per cent of those with no formal qualifications (Department of Employment 1992). Indeed, the buoyant demand for admission to IHEs has led the Conservative government to change its funding formula in order to slow the rate of expansion.[10]

The commitment of Conservative governments for over a decade to the ideology of the free market, and to a reduction in public expenditure, has effectively ruled out any significant injection of new public monies to finance expansion in the way in which it was undertaken following the Robbins Report in the 1960s (Kogan 1983). In the early 1990s, this led to the creation of a quasi-market within which institutions of higher education compete for students and resources (Ainley and Vickerstaff, forthcoming). Hence, in order to create a "level playing field" (to use the contemporary jargon) the costs per student, which had previously been greater in the established universities than in the polytechnics, were standardized (at the lower prices) and the binary system was abolished, with the former polytechnics renamed as universities. The creation of a single market for higher education (with the exception of some colleges of higher education) has forced all universities to expand student numbers in order to survive.[11] They have accepted the need to reduce unit costs if the governments previous target of one third of the 18-21 age range in some sort of higher education is to be attained by the year 2000. There are now more than one million full- and part-time, home and overseas students in higher education in Britain, of which 40 per cent are female, excluding the student nurse population. Half of the student body are outside the 18-21 age range and many now live at home during their studies (Bourner 1991). Approximately 13 per cent are postgraduates, whose numbers increased by 65 per cent throughout the 1980s. This growth in numbers entering higher education has been achieved despite the introduction of loans to compensate for the declining value of student grants. Flat-rate fees paid via local education authorities to higher education institutions have also been differentiated by subject area in an attempt by the government to encourage more students to study science and technology in preference to the more popular arts and social sciences subjects. This may well lead some institutions to charge "top-up" fees for their more popular courses. Such fees and loans may be seen as undermining the Robbins principle of free higher education, yet as Ball (1990) asserts:

> Access by competition to a scarce good always favours the privileged: women, ethnic minorities, lower socio-economic groups and the handicapped lose out. The solution is to de-ration higher education by charging higher fees, to be met (at least in part) from private sources, and to arrange for students to make a greater contribution towards the cost of their own maintenance. (p. 752)[12]

The introduction of a quasi-market in higher education may yet be further augmented by the mechanism of a voucher entitlement to post-compulsory education or training, which is congruent with the expansion of market choice within primary and secondary schooling (Chitty 1989, Brown 1990). At first sight this apparent democratization of higher education appears to be consistent with a technical functional view of a post-industrial workforce, and to an increasing deregulation of talent as more non-traditional students gain a university education. However, there seems no doubt that "more" means "different" (Ball 1990). It is highly likely that, with research increasingly concentrated in "centres of excellence", a new binary divide may emerge as many universities at the bottom end of the hierarchy become teaching-only institutions. Here "skills" courses narrowly related to employment will be concentrated, along with perhaps two-year – as opposed to three- and four-year – degree programmes. At the same time there will be other courses of a less vocational nature to serve the "cultural" needs of students from more privileged backgrounds, who will ultimately obtain employment in a broad range of intellectual, artistic and conceptually-orientated occupations (Ainley 1993).

Moreover, rather than contemplate the prospect of further increases in student numbers, some of the established universities may seek to increase the costs of study, which will force students to pay top-up fees and impose financial as well as academic entry requirements to preserve their "elite" status. In 1993, the London School of Economics (which is part of the University of London) proposed the introduction of top-up fees of between £500 and £1,000 for all courses, but this proposal has since been rejected. Nevertheless, the introduction of a new funding system for higher education, requiring students to pay towards their tuition and subsistence now seems to be inevitable (Committee of Vice-Chancellors and Principals (CVCP) 1993).[13] Whatever funding system is introduced, as the number of graduates increases there is unlikely to be any shortage of middle-class families willing to convert their material capital into cultural capital in order to gain a competitive advantage by gaining a graduate qualification from an "elite" institution.

Claims to an increasingly democratized system of higher education also include the assumption that the increasing emphasis on the vocational rôle of higher education necessitates a shift away from academic elitism. This is especially noticeable in the emphasis on personal and transferable skills in an era of "adaptive" organizational paradigms. In these, employers recognize the need for dynamic individuals able to move flexibly within the organization, and who are able to build up a portfolio of transferable expertise in the course of a career, and who are able to work effectively in interdepartmental teams. At the Annual Conference of the Society for Research in Higher Education, Ann Bailey articulated the present position of many large and medium sized employers in calling on higher education to produce "well rounded individuals" with good personal and transferable skills. The implications for the recruitment of graduates into organizations such as the high-tech company which Bailey (1990) represented, demonstrates the increased importance now attached to personal and social skills:

> Even where there is an established set of criteria against which to sift applicants, selection of candidates for interview is often carried out as a "gut-feeling" reaction to the quality of the application. If the students have recognized the necessity of a curriculum vitae as a means to - "sell" themselves and have learned how to produce one, they will score highly on measures of capability. (p. 70)

"Measures of capability" sound impressively objective but "gut-feelings" are immeasurable, cultural, tacit knowledge, although decisive in interviews in which "applicants will have to demonstrate that these life/personal skills are not just 'head knowledge' but an integral part of themselves" (Bailey 1990; 70). These so-called "personal, transferable skills" are required in a variety of work situations rendered increasingly similar through the introduction of information technology and new forms of work organization (Ainley 1993).

At rock bottom, the real skills for employment presented as "personable and transferable" involve the exhibition of middle-class cultural capital, not only manifest indirectly through academic qualifications, but also directly through the development of the appropriate socio-emotional features of middle-class identities (see Chapter 6). These are the truly generic social skills that are most acceptable to most employers. Indeed, a flick through a few graduate brochures confirms this impression. The cultural change of the new adaptive employing organizations may thus result in little more than a reassertion of these traditional, though more explicit, virtues. Although examination success is necessary for entry to most managerial and professional occupations, it no longer provides (in so far as it ever did) the sole criteria for selection and promotion which, in the manner of the "charismatic" qualities now required for the new forms of "team working", are attested by indefinable "personal qualities", so that, as employers admit, they tend to recruit people like themselves, whom they can "trust". Against such tacit discrimination for selection and promotion there is, of course, no resort to the formal procedures of appeal that were at least a part of the bureaucratic hierarchy, since there are fewer criteria upon which to base such claims.

Skills such as team working, familiarity with information technology and with the main European languages are becoming integrated with subject teaching across the separate discipline cultures of higher education. This is more the case where subjects of study are combined, through modularity for example, than in traditional, single subject courses. It is through the informal curricula of campus and college activities that students acquire much of what they learn at university, beyond the often specialized and limited technical expertise or factual and theoretical knowledge of their particular subject of study. The absence of such extracurricular activities at new universities is compensated for by the addition of "skills" courses to the formal curriculum. The so-called "personal transferable skills" are then taught separately from the culture of which they form a part, because personal and transferable skills are inherently social and generic. Therefore efforts to acquire these social and generic skills by formal teaching, rather than as part of the culture of the informal curricula of college and campus, could result in an opposite effect to that intended. To present attitudes and habits dignified as skills and technical abilities that can be acquired piecemeal by practice and study not only divorces them from their real cultural context but also represents them as being equally accessible to all students whatever their class, cultural background, gender or race. It ignores the fact that middle-class students already possess many of these personal "qualities" as a result of their previous education and family socialization. As Bourdieu and Passeron (1977) have pointed out, even if middle-class students do not already have all of these social abilities, their previous experience lays the foundations upon which to build them.[14]

Hence, although the emphasis on personal and transferable skills may be viewed as contributing to a fundamental change in the nature of higher education, the established universities have shown little enthusiasm for social skills training. History provides a plausible explanation, for although the new universities have attuned themselves to the needs of industry, the established universities are believed to recruit the most talented students. Therefore the fact that the established universities have not responded to the demands of employers paradoxically serves to enhance the job opportunities of their students. Indeed, in the context of rapid technological innovation and market uncertainty, the demonstration of high calibre is more important than the acquisition of applied skills, because much of what is learnt is soon out of date. In a society where standards of excellence have been defined and symbolized by the elite universities, especially Oxbridge, graduate employers maintain a cognitive map which places Oxford and Cambridge Universities at the apex, and work down. A Mori opinion poll asked industrialists, teachers and members of the general public to list their top ten universities. Only twelve names featured on the three lists. None of the (now established) post-Robbins universities were mentioned by any of those interviewed.

In this context, the development of formal personal and social skills training in less prestigious institutions takes the form of a "deficit model"; it is for those who do not already possess, or acquire, the necessary cultural distinction during the normal course of their experience in higher education, which access to superior jobs increasingly demands.

Despite the predictions that can be made based upon present tendencies, it is important to appreciate that neither the form that the

Table 3.1   Top ten universities.

Managers in industry and commerce

1. Cambridge	6. Manchester
2. Oxford	7. Edinburgh
3. London	8. Durham
4. Birmingham	9. Leeds
5. Bristol	10. Southampton

Teachers

1. Cambridge	6. Manchester
2. Oxford	7. Birmingham and Edinburgh
3. Bristol	9. Exeter
4. Durham	10. Nottingham
5. London	

General public

1. Cambridge	6. Bristol
2. Oxford	7. Durham
3. London	8. Birmingham
4. Edinburgh	9. Exeter
5. Manchester	No other universities registered on the measure used

latest extension of higher education to a larger proportion of the population will take, nor its curricular content, is firmly established. It may be recalled that the previous, more limited expansion of higher education led to a reassessment of education policy following the student unrest of the late 1960s. As much as anything else, this was a product of frustrated expectations that greater access to higher education would lead to new and more demanding job opportunities. With continued economic stagnation, the same frustration is likely to recur, only this time, if present targets are reached, for far larger number of graduates. Too many variables make impossible any prophecy as to what form this frustration will take this time around. For one thing, the previous student radicalization took place in the context of continued, if fitful, economic expansion. Now there is a public acceptance of high rates of unemployment, and a significant minority of university graduates in the 1990s will inevitably fail to find a job after graduation (see Table 3.2).

Table 3.2   Unemployment rates.

Year	Average (%)	Graduate (%)
1987	10.0	6.9
1988	8.1	5.8
1989	6.3	5.2
1990	5.8	8.2
1991	8.1	11.5
1992	9.9	14.5

Source: Observer, 29 August 1993.

On the other hand, the situation of students in an education system that has traditionally separated learning from living, and knowledge from action, is inherently contradictory so that, as Boddington (1978) recorded, "The most deeply rooted crisis is in the consciousness of students, in schools as well as in universities" (p. 82). This is because, as he explained,

> education is a social attempt deliberately and consciously to impart knowledge and enlarge the capacity for acquiring knowledge . . . Knowledge and imagination are vital to the effective functioning of the social system [and] "Advanced industry needs to 'socialise' scientific exploration" [but] The very nature of knowledge and imagination contradicts attempts to make them completely subservient to the existing social order . . . They reveal new possibilities . . . So [that] social knowledge is always liable to overstep the bounds of the society by which it is generated. (pp. 80, 84).

The attempt to resolve this contradiction between general knowledge and its particular application is only partly resolved by the recent emphasis upon the vocational relevance of higher education because this raises expectations for employment that in a changed organizational, economic and cultural context cannot be met for most graduates.[16] In the short term, the changed demands upon graduate labour that have accompanied the cultural changes in employing organizations place higher education and its staff and students in new relationships with the conventional professional careers previously secured by a higher education. Such bureaucratic certainties, prepared for and attested by traditional learning and examination, are increasingly called into question by the insistence upon personal qualities of flexibility and risk-taking for a "career" in reorganized private and public employment.

There are, then, a number of fundamental changes occurring in the relationship between higher education and graduate careers. The perceptions of the rôle of universities in a modern economy are being redefined both by employing organizations and participating university students. Clearly, the growth of higher education has reinforced differentiated educational experiences as these are encountered within different universities. From our preceding discussion, it is evident that it is possible to distinguish an academic hierarchy within which there are at least three strata, although not formally designated in higher education policy. First, there are Oxford and Cambridge (and possibly London) Universities, which continue to constitute elite establishments with the highest requirements for entry and which play a crucial rôle in the cultural reproduction of social elites. Secondly, there are other established universities set up from the late 19th century until the end of the 1960s, which have grown in response to the changing technological, managerial and cultural demands of the occupational structure. Finally, there are the "new" universities, created from the polytechnics in the 1990s, which are more vocationally-orientated and which have traditionally tailored their curricula to the "needs" of industry.

In view of these differences, it would hardly be surprising if there were not differences in the perceptions of both students and employing organizations as to the worth of higher education as well as the cultural and material value of university study as this is pursued in each of the three types of institution mentioned above. Hence, in order to explore this issue we undertook a small but in-depth, empirical survey of student attitudes. We began with a consideration of how far students from a broad range of social backgrounds and educational experiences share the conception of a market for academic merit, in which their position in the educational hierarchy and subsequent occupational opportunities (or lack of them) are justified by equal access to, and opportunities for, educational achievement.

In 1990 a pilot questionnaire was administered at three English universities "Oxbridge", "Home Counties" and "Inner City" (one being at that time a former polytechnic) in order to examine the range of educational experiences and occupational expectations of undergraduates in their final year of study.[17] Oxbridge was chosen because it stands at the apex of the academic hierarchy. The predominance of this institution is reflected in its size as well as the wealth of many of its colleges.[18] But with more than 10,000 undergraduate students within the university as a whole, many of the self-governing Oxbridge colleges are as large as single universities elsewhere, and because of this pre-eminent position, Oxbridge represents the most complete example of "the traditional ideal of the English university". As such, Oxbridge has been "crucial in forming the values of the English model of a university to which the rest of the system of higher education has aspired" (Salter and Tapper 1992). As the Master of Kings College tells the eponymous hero of Robert McLiam Wilson's (1989) novel *Ripley Bogle* before expelling him from the College:

> No-one is greater than this university. Goodness no, it is much too old and has seen far to much for that. Whether you liked it or not, when you came to Cambridge you signed yourself up as a member of an elite. An elite, mind you – meritocracy, aristocracy – it matters little. Still an elite. Egalitarians don't come to Cambridge. (pp. 210-11).

This elite status immediately strikes visitors and new students who find the river lined by ancient college buildings and walled gardens. The ivy-clad, mullioned facade signals the presence of privilege as clearly as anywhere in England. Students feel the presence, and in their gowns, feel part of an elite group, glimpsed by visitors down narrow alleys and through Gothic archways opening into cobbled courtyards. The University thus exerts a subtle pressure of long-established permanency and importance upon its visitors and students alike.

Home Counties is another established university which has buoyant demand for most of its degree programmes, especially from middle-class students living in the Midlands and the South of England. A large proportion of the 6000 students live on campus. In comparison to Oxbridge, the academic status of Home Counties is modest, although it is recognized as a suitable place for middle class families to send their children. Rather like the ancient foundations of Oxford and Cambridge, the universities founded in the 1960s "were built, like the medieval cathedrals, for ever, to the glory of God, and for the admiration of the peasantry without regard to their public pocket" (Halsey 1992a, 7). Thus Home Counties University stands as a monument to faded establishment aspirations to unite the Arts and Sciences in its social and academic organization. Spread over a large campus, it represents an attempt to transplant in modern concrete a smaller clone of Oxbridge. In this respect it resembles its academic inhabitants, many of whom moved from the elite universities in the expansion of the profession during the 1960s. Such was, in Halsey's phrase, "the grip of the ancient over the modern" (1992a, 17), that it was natural for Oxbridge-trained academics to move from teaching the single-subject honours degrees associated with the 19th-century civic universities of London and the industrial North of England, back towards the Oxbridge organization of multisubject schools, presenting the choice and integration of study that this allowed as a curricular innovation. Thus Home Counties, like the seven other "new" universities built in the heyday of postwar university expansion, made, as Halsey (1992a) suggests, "the label that they received in the 1960s meaningless".

Inner City has recently gained university status following the demise of the binary system in 1992. It has expanded rapidly since the early 1970s, following the merger of a number of separate technical and further education colleges scattered over three separate inner city boroughs. Many of its 9000 students live locally in a world socially and culturally far removed from the sheltered groves of ancient and modern academe. A large number of students study on a part-time basis and the university actively seeks to attract women, ethnic minorities and mature students. The vast majority of Inner City students are from manual, working-class backgrounds, and have maintained strong community ties. The general level of disadvantage in the area is evident in the fact that it has one of the lowest take-up rates for higher education in the country.

On the basis of our pilot study it became obvious that the kind of data we wanted to explore required a series of in-depth interviews with students and employers. Initially, twenty final year students from both Oxbridge and Home Counties were interviewed in 1990–1. In the following academic year a further 50 students were interviewed at Home Counties. All the Oxbridge and Home Counties interviews were chosen to reflect the appropriate number of female and male students across the various subject disciplines. They also largely conformed to the stereotypical 18–21 year old, traditionally middle-class student. This cross-section was compared with a sample of 50 full-time students attending Inner City University. A large proportion of those interviewed were female and from ethnic minority backgrounds, which largely reflected the composition of the student population. However, because they were selected from those whose term-time address was the same as their permanent address, mature students were over-represented. Conventional students from Oxbridge and Home Counties Universities were thus contrasted with these "new" students, more of whom will have to be attracted to university if government targets of up to one third of the 18–21 age group, plus adult learners and returners, are to enter a mass higher education system within the next decade. In addition, the respondents also provided pedagogical polarities, from largely traditional, academic courses and modes of assessment at Oxbridge and Home Counties Universities, to modular and independent study at Inner City. Inner City University also offers a greater variety of subjects for study, in which applied sciences and technology predominate, and of degree and non-degree courses.

The comparison between these three universities affords an opportunity to compare student perceptions of their position within an academic hierarchy of IHEs; what they thought they had learnt while at university; how they felt differences in social background affect their experiences of higher education; and their orientations to the labour market at a time of corporate restructuring. These issues are discussed in Chapters 4 and 5. A further empirical question is whether employers are changing their perceptions of graduate entrants and hence their recruitment strategies. Do they recognize a significant shift away from bureaucratic organizational structures? Has this involved a change in the nature of managerial competence and the kinds of graduate they are looking to recruit into "fast-track" training programmes? To what extent will changes in employer recruitment practices reinforce class, gender and racial inequalities in access to professional and managerial work? In order to explore these questions, we spoke to 30 graduate recruiters in 16 large and medium-sized organizations – mainly in the private sector – in banking, accounting, pharmaceuticals, electrical engineering, and information technology. These organizations are not necessarily representative of all graduate employers, given that a growing number of graduates are being recruited by smaller organizations. It is also fair to say that virtually all the recruiters we spoke to offered high quality training, which cannot be said of all organizations who employ graduates. These issues of employer recruitment strategies are discussed in Chapter 6.

The issues addressed in the last of the empirical chapters – Chapter 7 – focus on how student perceptions of work and future life chances have changed as a result of their initial experiences of employment. To what extent have their experiences led to positive and negative feelings about working life in the 1990s? How have they coped with the transition from university to the labour market? To what extent is work a central life interest and a source of self-fulfilment? To gain a sense of graduates' initial responses to working life we conducted 20 in-depth interviews with students graduating from the three institutions approximately 18 months after completing their undergraduate studies. By concentrating on those who were in employment we attempted to assess the impact of corporate restructuring on graduate recruitment and student orientations to work. However, with significant numbers of students either unemployed or who have been forced to "trade down" into non-graduate jobs, there is clearly an urgent need for future research to explore the implications of unmet expectations at a time when graduate numbers are increasing.

Much of the argument in this book must inevitably be speculative, given that the empirical fieldwork was conducted shortly before the end of the binary divide within higher education in 1992. Moreover, the nature of corporate restructuring remains unclear at the time of writing and it may be some time before the full extent of these changes are reflected in patterns of graduate recruitment. Similarly, it is difficult to evaluate the full impact of the changing labour market conditions for graduates and their orientations to work and careers. In many respects, the argument presented in this book takes the form of a hypothesis rather than an empirical confirmation or refutation of clearly defined research questions. Therefore, the empirical data that informs this study is used for illustrative purposes, in the hope that it will encourage more systematic analysis of what we regard as vital questions concerning education, work organization and social stratification.

Notes

1. Hugh Trevor-Roper, Address to the Joint Association of Classical Teachers, reprinted in *The Spectator*, 14 July 1973. The early industrial

revolution was, as Eric Hobsbawm recorded, "technically rather primi-
tive", so that, as Landes (1968, 51) added, "at the middle of the nine-
teenth century, technology was still essentially empirical and on-the-job
training was in most cases the most effective means of communicating
skills. But once science began to anticipate technique – and it was already
doing so to some extent in the 1850s – formal education became a major industrial resource".

2. Moreover, the Trevelyan–Northcote reform of the civil service in 1854
   introduced competitive examination closely modelled upon the Oxbridge
   honours papers.
3. Higher education was seen as a means of gaining access to the market for
   professional "manpower", which in turn bestowed status upon the profession as well as its entrants (Glass 1959).
4. It is also worth noting that the Industrial Revolution in Britain was not
   achieved through the development of formal codified knowledge, but by
   "trial and error" inventors (see Green 1990). Management in Britain has
   been characterized in terms of the cult of the amateur who has achieved
   management status by climbing the internal labour market rather than
   through formal academic study.
5. For a discussion of the dominance of Oxford and Cambridge Universities and their enduring connections to the political, legal, civil service and
   business elites, see also Salter and Tapper 1992, Scott 1991).
6. Oxford and Cambridge thus became, as Perkin (1989) states, "the main
   articulator of the social idea of the professional class".
7. This built upon the previous monastic ideal of abstract contemplation and
   the Ancient Greek scorn for slave labour.
8. Smithers and Robinson, "A numerical picture of higher education",
   quoted in Manchester University Students Union *Papers on students rights*,
   Manchester, November 1991.
9. In 1990 there were 200,000 full-time male, and 151,000 female students
   (Halsey 1992b).
10. The social engine of this expansion is plainly to be found in the new
    middle of society where the previously clear-cut distinction between the
    non-manual middle class and the manual working-class has been eroded
    by the growth of services, especially in offices and selling. The latest
    applications of new technology have also replaced many of the hard
    labouring jobs of the past (Ainley 1993). These changes reflect a process
    of wider economic and social "restructuring", discussed in earlier chap-
    ters.
11. The universities reliance upon state funding meant the loss of their much-
    cherished but largely illusory independence. Despite "the concept of
    autonomy" being, as Salter and Tapper (1992) remark, "central to . . . the

traditional idea of the university", "only the most perverse re-reading of history could claim that the British universities remained autonomous institutions by the final days of the University Grants Council" (p. 228). In higher education, the creation of a market has been aided by the fact that the established universities were semi-autonomous institutions with control over their own budgets. The removal of the binary divide between universities and polytechnics in 1992 removed the latter from the control of local education authorities to whom they had previously been accountable. Moreover, in the 1980s the established universities responded to the cuts in funding that were imposed upon them, by "raising the grades they required for entry rather than squeezing in all those who met previously acceptable standards" (Fulton 1991). In the 1990s this is no longer a viable option.

12. Ball (1990) goes on to say that "However, targeted help must be available for the needy" (p. 752).

13. The proposed introduction of top-up fees at the London School of Economics was reported in the *Independent on Sunday*, 6 June 1993.

14. Old cultural distinctions rendered increasingly arbitrary by their lack of correspondence with rapidly changing material circumstances can still be preserved by the selection of a minority through an antique and academic curriculum. In this case the facility of new technology for reducing cultural qualities to arbitrary quantities can be used to produce elaborate and supposedly objective rank orderings of individuals in a reanimated hierarchy. Then, as Laborit observed, "the more the hierarchical system is staggered and individualized, the greater the sovereignty of the commodity" (Laborit 1977, 153; Ainley 1993).

15. Reported in the *Guardian*, 16 May 1989. The article does not give any details about sample size or composition. Obviously such evidence needs to be treated with caution, but the fact that Cambridge and Oxford are at the top of all three lists and only 12 universities get a mention is significant.

16. Whatever the outcome of the new accommodation between higher education and employment, the current expansion of higher education poses cultural questions that are fundamental to the survival of the arts, sciences, and their application in technologies as expressions of the unique human ability to imagine and hence alter its future, and thus to the survival of the species (Stanley 1978).

17. Two hundred and fifty questionnaires were obtained, which included 100 each from Oxbridge and Home Counties and 50 from an inner city polytechnic not used in the detailed study.

18. Gilbert Ryles (1963) *The concept of mind* explains the concept of Oxford and Cambridge in the following terms:

A foreigner visiting Oxford or Cambridge for the first time is shown a number of colleges, libraries, playing fields, museums, scientific departments and administrative offices. He then asks, "But where is the University? I have seen where the members of the Colleges live, where the Registrar works, where the scientists experiment and the rest. But I have not yet seen the University in which reside and work the members of your University." It has then to be explained to him that the University is not another collateral institution, some ulterior counterpart to the colleges, laboratories and offices which he has seen. The University is just the way in which all that he has already seen is organized. When they are seen and when their coordination is understood, the University has been seen. (pp. 17-18)

Moreover, Oxbridge is celebrated by the media as the evergreen world of "glittering prizes". Although, as Salter and Tapper (1992) remark, the image of "Brideshead Revisited is not an Oxbridge that many of todays dons find attractive". Nevertheless, this image of Oxbridge remains "an essential part of the status symbolism of British elites" (Halsey and Trow 1971, pp. 206-7).

CHAPTER FOUR

Social divisions of learning

What students learn at university serves both as a preparation for employment and as a cultural apprenticeship for their anticipated or confirmed class status. It is this "social" education, in addition to the specialized knowledge they also acquire, that is explored in this chapter. In particular, we are interested in the relationship between academic achievement and the class cultural identities of students. We also explore the value they attach to their educational experiences and how they locate themselves within the hierarchy of the more highly educated.

In Bourdieu's and Passeron's (1964) study of higher education in France, they suggest that the "university tradition offers the student two major models, apparently contradictory but equally approved, the 'exam-hound' and the 'dilettante'" (p.57). The former concentrates upon "obsessive swotting" to achieve "the examination pass that has become his [or her] sole goal", while what the authors describe as "the ideology of effortless achievement" supports the ideal of achieving the highest pass without any apparent effort. Both these "model" students ascribed to what Bourdieu and Passeron call the "cult of the grade". "The grade" has come to assume even greater importance to virtually all the students in our study.

Even where there is emphasis upon additional benefits of the course beyond those accredited for an final examination mark, it is the final result that counts with these students. This is shown clearly by their reluctance to attend courses that offer experiences which will not be formally credited, or to read any books or perform any experiments that will not be examined. The rationale behind this instrumental view of their university studies is not difficult to understand. For most students the "credential nexus" of compliance for good grades had already worked successfully for most of them in gaining entry to university. They are also fully aware that a graduate qualification is a basic requirement for obtaining better paid and more prestigious jobs, irrespective of whether they have decided what kind of vocation to pursue. Moreover, the impact of economic recession has been to reinforce rather than weaken these instrumental orientations to university life. The cult of the grade at times of bleak job prospects is more than an amusing competition among peers; it is an attempt to gain personal advantage in the competition for scarce job opportunities. The importance attached to examination success was evident among female and male students alike in all three institutions:

> I came here to get a degree. I did consider going into, like, retail management or something instead, but basically I wanted a career in Electronic Engineering so I came here to get the qualification to go for it, so that's been the main motivation.

> Qualifications in themselves are a means to an end, they are instrumental rather than intrinsic . . . you come to university to get a degree and it's as a degree holder that you're going to get on. It's like the difference between being an NCO in the Army and being an Officer. You can only go so far, whereas being a commissioned officer the sky's the limit. I think you can look at it in that sort of parallel as it were . . .

> The reason then is it would give me better job prospects, at the time, you know, that was when there was almost two and a half times the inflation . . . [and] unemployment . . . Any, anything to give me the edge would be an advantage.

> I never really thought about it in terms of going to study my subject further. I came to university really because it was a means to an end, it would get me where I wanted to be in terms of a career. That was the real reason I came.

> That is the reason for being here. I've not come for self-development or survival. I came here to get the means for a passport.

> To get a degree to open as many doors as possible. A piece of paper.

I wasn't looking for more than that because I've already experienced the wider world.

However, it was at the two established universities that the pressure of examination success was felt more acutely, given the overriding importance attached to the end of year examinations and especially the "finals", in which a students three years at university are judged primarily on the basis of his/her performance in the examination hall over a period lasting little more than two weeks. At Home Counties, "finals" were sat in both the second and third years, whereas at Oxbridge they were often concentrated at the end of the third year.

The intense sense of competition which accompanied traditional written examinations in Oxbridge was felt to be potentially damaging by some interviewees: "The thing that really got me was the huge competitiveness at exam time which took over completely, more than the value of the exams. It does a lot to damage people."

Female students seem to be more aware of this intense competition than the men. However, they did not appear to feel disadvantaged. Gender, indeed, figured in a strangely inverted manner in students assessment of their academic attainments, with some women in all three institutions commenting on the advantages, as they perceived them, of being an exceptional minority in typically male subjects such as science. The reverse was not the case for males in predominantly female subjects, such as languages, where the minority of men undoubtedly do enjoy advantages (Thomas 1990). Students also seemed unaware of the well-established "clumping" of final examination classifications by gender, with females typically achieving second class honours degrees while males were likely to get either a first or third class degree (Rudd 1984).[1]

Although the cult of the grade is uppermost in the minds of many students, the means to academic success reveal sharp differences among students, as does their sense of "being" in higher education. The tradition of "effortless achievement" derives from an elite upper stratum that could and still can afford to have its offspring educated privately and intensively from an early age. The purpose of such an education was succinctly explained by the headteacher of one of Britains leading private schools:

I am not paid to get boys into a polytechnic; nor am I paid to get them into any university. I am paid to get them into a good univer-

57

sity, and preferably Oxford or Cambridge. And I do a jolly good job (quoted in Nuttgens 1988, 125).

As they progress through a succession of nannies, preparatory and boarding schools to an extended childhood at sheltered colleges and finishing schools, achievement in this system appears natural, if not always effortless (Wakeford 1969). The familiarity of middle-class students with the general milieu of higher education accounts for the fact that students from professional and managerial backgrounds found university life, and their academic studies, much as they had anticipated. Thus, as these female and male interviewees from middle-class backgrounds, most of whom were at Oxbridge recalled:

I'd been brought up to go to university really . . . the school I went to is very much geared to sending people to university, especially Oxbridge, they like to send about 15 or so people every year . . . I don't suppose it was a real conscious decision, it was something I did because it was expected and because it was a natural thing to do.

To a large extent it was the kind of thing that was expected of me by my school, by my parents and my teachers, and I remember that it had always been expected that I would go to university if I was clever enough and that I would go to Oxbridge.

I went to a grammar school in Tunbridge. I remember the day, I remember the conversation when I was eleven years old as to whether I should go to Oxbridge. At the time it didn't really strike me as important.

I went to grammar school where it was almost the accepted norm . . . the next step along. My parents both went to university and it was the obvious thing to do . . . I actually grew up down the road and was trained in the chapel choir in Oxbridge.

My parents are both teachers . . . and obviously I would go to university. At secondary school it became obvious that I would get the chance to go to Oxbridge, and again, there wasn't any reason not to do that.

You know if you even *breathed* the notion, the notion of leaving school and getting married and having babies you were instantly garrotted and also you know, I worked out for myself that that was probably what was best for me. But I didn't come straight here [Home Counties], I took a year off which was something I really felt I had to do. I wasn't *very* happy at school, even though I knew that I, I wanted *eventually* to go to university, um, I wanted to do my own thing for a while so I took a year off and did various things and, and then I was *ready* to come to university . . .

Given such advantages and opportunities, "you just don't say 'no' basically, that's what it comes down to." Thus, "the accumulation of intellectual achievements", as Simmel (1978, 442) noted, "gives a rapidly growing and disproportionate advantage to those who are favoured by it [so that] the highest stages of education require less effort for every step further than the lower stages, and yet at the same time produce greater results".[2] The social and educational advantages enjoyed by middle class students were clearly recognized by students from working-class origins at Home Counties and Inner City:

I think from the financial point of view, that you need the support of your parents in terms of parental contributions and grants or support while you are at university, to go back home during the vacations, to be dependent on your parents; that depends upon their economic position, which ultimately is going to be down to their social class, occupation. Perhaps working-class families wouldn't be able, you know, to let their children go to university even if they had the ability and the qualifications because they didn't feel they could support them when they came home in the vacation or while they were away. Whereas, if it was sort of middle-class, then their parents probably would have expect it from an early age, and planned that their children should go to university, put money aside for their childrens education, and saw it as a predictable and natural thing to happen. Whereas I think the working-class families, they don't necessarily expect their children to go to university, and I don't think it's something that they plan.

I mean, I am sort of from a working-class family and OK none of my family have been to university or anything and you know my fathers a gardener for the council so . . . and where I live I suppose in some ways you're just expected to leave school. It's against the norm to carry on in higher education, not many of my friends from home have done, and so . . . that I suppose can restrict you from getting on. And also it seems, you know, your background, who you know, things like that seem to [matter] . . . who your father knows.

However, even though some Oxbridge students acknowledged that their social backgrounds had given them a competitive edge, they regarded their progress and academic achievement, reflected in their final degree awards, as being achieved through meritocratic competition. They were encouraged in this by their teachers at both school and university for, as Robinson (1968) has pointed out:

> In academic circles the type and class of degree tend to be used not as a measure of the level of education attained but as an indication of the academic quality of the individual. The academic world believes in the concept of innate ability; it believes that people have distinct levels of ability indicated by the type of first degree obtained – a man is an ordinary degree man or a first class man [sic]. (p. 78)

It is for this reason that "mature" students, who enter by non-conventional routes, such as Access courses or via BTEC examinations, often feel disadvantaged by comparison with the standard full-time "A" level entrants (Bourner et al. 1991). Even though the official university entrance policy encouraged such applicants to apply, as one mature student at Home Counties expressed it: "People who've done "A" levels seemed to be more acceptable to come to university. You really feel a bit of an underdog. The other students make you feel you've got something to prove, not the staff – they didn't know." As a result, they often feel that they "got in through the back door" and "did not deserve to be there". Consequently, they could not believe their "luck", and one mature woman entrant, for instance, recalled how when she first arrived, "I wandered around in a dream for days, pinching myself. I couldn't believe it was really me here . . . The place didn't seem made for people like me."

The question of social confidence among students was closely related to differences in cultural capital. The middle-class students at Oxbridge and Home Counties were very much at home in a university environment. They took their experiences of higher education for granted since this is what had been expected of them from an early age. This was less the case for working-class students, young and old alike, who had come from families and schools where it was unusual to progress beyond secondary education. Indeed, a number of students from working-class backgrounds have had to come to terms with the fact that going to university has involved a psychological and social distancing from families and friends, but that it has also left them ill-at-ease within the new world they have entered, as this male student from Home Counties explained:

> I thought I'd meet a really elite set of academic people . . . I was a bit anxious that they'd probably be well above me and I'd be out of my depth here, at least that's what I was told by my friends before I came here . . . there is a distinct kind of class difference here, there's a lot of people from well-to-do families . . . I was surprised at the amount of people there from that kind of environment, with their own values . . . these . . . people think they're better than they actually are, because in reality I don't think they are any better, apart from they have got that much more money, but there seems to be this thing about . . . the way you express yourself, carry yourself, um, an accent . . . they're quite happy to think that ethic, could be a class ethic, or whatever, which is a bit of a piss off . . . but that's the general tone. You can sit in the SCR all day and you can tick it off, you can feel it.

Similarly, at Inner City the interviewees who had overcome seemingly insuperable difficulties to enter higher education and complete their studies – including cases of illness and house eviction, as well as family and educational backgrounds that had hardly prepared them for further study – were sometimes still troubled by a chronic lack of confidence and felt that they did not "deserve" the often excellent passes they had received. Recognising such "hidden injuries of class" (Sennett and Cobb 1977) as the result of childhood and schooling did not make them easier to overcome. For instance, this female student noted:

> Because of when I was younger I've really got no confidence in myself. It's more than my school experience; it's my home life because I had a very unhappy childhood . . . I don't know what you call it but I felt I had a bit of a gap in my education and I wanted to broaden myself. I felt a bit narrow. I'm glad I've got the degree, 'cos if I didn't do the degree I would've taken the easy way and gone on in sales and I didn't like sales work really. But now with the degree I look through the adverts every week and I don't know what I'm

going to do and also I don't feel as confident now as I did before . . .
I'm still making up my mind, I haven't decided what it is I want to
do. I'd like to do some tutoring and I've applied to the local Further
Education College but I think it's a bit out of my depth.

The lack of the appropriate cultural capital exhibited by working-
class students when they entered university made it extremely difficult for them to exhibit "effortless achievement". Indeed, the
working-class dilettante usually ends up dropping out of university![3]
Social confidence among working-class students was derived through
academic success, and being an "exam-hound" was a vital part of their
cultural apprenticeship. It was through examination success, even if
this did not amount to "first-class" grades, that working-class students
felt they deserved to be at university on their own merits.

Therefore, it is perhaps not surprising that "confidence" was what
many students felt they had gained from their higher education, and
"confidence", as John Kenny once stated, "breeds competence" (in
Ainley 1991). Whether this was merely the confidence of being able
to say "I went to Oxbridge or Inner City University", or the hard-won
confidence to engage with literature and in conversation that had been
lacking before, the power that education conferred was more immediately apparent to student interviewees of working-class origin than
to those who already took it for granted. To some of these working-
class students the element of a cultural apprenticeship and a growth
in social confidence was evident:

> It was almost like a religious experience, going from working in a
> factory and being unemployed to be told you can get to university.
> I thought they were taking the piss, quite honestly. I just looked on
> it as a year away from work and then the confidence just sort of hits
> you as you're going through it and people are starting to take you
> seriously as a thinking person – lecturers and qualified professional
> people.

> It was a really good course for introducing you to names that are
> always bandied about by people – Marx and Freud and people – and
> unless you study them, I felt I would never get any understanding
> of what they were on about and I kind of feel now that I've got the
> confidence to go further if I wanted to, whereas if I hadn't studied
> them on my course I wouldn't dream of picking up one of their
> books.

Working-class students, who are more likely to enter a new university such as Inner City, often found their studies to be more demanding than they had anticipated. They therefore worked harder than the other interviewees, spending longer in libraries, laboratories, formal classes and seminars, where they were more intensively taught in order, as their lecturers sometimes told them, to "bring them up to scratch". As a result, despite poorer facilities, more of them than the Oxbridge and Home Counties university students were familiar with the use of new technology, both for word processing and with the statistical applications of various computer packages. These abilities, of course, are prominent among those "personal and transferable skills" universally listed by employers in their requirements of graduate recruits. Such technical skills were not, however, listed among the personal or "charismatic" qualities that many students appreciated were sought by employers for the more prestigious graduate jobs.

Subject of study was considered irrelevant to what most of the Home Counties and Oxbridge students thought they had learnt on campus. They often felt that they had learnt more outside the context of formal study, in student societies and with the friends that took up so much of their time on campus or in college. As one Oxbridge interviewee recorded, "the two main purposes of university are to obtain a degree and have a social life". While the latter is the more enjoyable it is no less educationally essential, though recognized only indirectly as such:

> I think the main skill that you learn at university is awareness, different ways of looking at things, particularly in a sociology course. Really, to be given information and to be able to evaluate it and come up with certain conclusions, but that's as far as it goes. I don't think you receive any training whatsoever that is directly relevant to employment. I mean we don't learn how to type or we don't learn how to . . . use computers unless it's integrated with a particular course . . . there isn't anything that's directly a work skill, that I can go into a market place and say this is what I've learnt . . . I think, in fact, what you've learnt from living alongside other people, other students, is a lot more valuable . . . you learn how to live with other people, how to compromise yourself, living for instance with three or four people, learn how to get on. You're responsible for yourself, you learn how to communicate better with people your own age, in

your particular situation, and help one another with problems. So I think . . . that's quite valuable.

The lack of a social life centred on campus and college was recognized by students from the two established universities and by some from Inner City University, as a social, if not academic, disadvantage of having to study while living at home, although for many of the Inner City interviewees this social disadvantage was outweighed by convenience, cost or force of circumstance. Mature students at Home Counties also regretted that their family and work commitments prevented them from participating more in campus activities. Among the skills which would undoubtedly be considered "personal and transferable", an Oxbridge student reported gaining from participation in informal, extracurricular activities:

> debating . . . presentation skills . . . persuading people . . . social skills . . . you grow up an awful lot . . . academic skills, working skills, applications skills . . . managing skills in being in charge of a society. You learn by learning. I had to organize, manage, delegate.

Another Oxbridge student stated that he had learnt as much solely by being "College Captain of Boats" for a year.

Whereas Oxbridge and Home Counties university students acquired such social skills through involvement in societies, on course committees and through the Students Union, Inner City students were less likely to do so because they lived at home and because societies and college social events played less of a part in their life generally. Yet, paradoxically, although they spent less time in formal study than those at Inner City, students from the two established universities reported that they learnt more. This was because being by and large of a younger age, the established university students learnt more "just as a result of growing up", "living away from home, coping", "learning to live with people my own age", so that "I've become more tolerant" [or] "I'm not so shy" [and] "I can cook now!". In this sense the university is experienced, just as it is often denigrated by critics, as a "finishing school" for middle-class youth. Though the younger students from Home Counties and Oxbridge reported benefits of living away from home for the first time, they also recognized that they were very sheltered because, "we're given accommodation and we live in a college and everything is within the college, I like not having to deal with those things." For students who live on campus or in college, this attitude is often encouraged by having domestic staff who make their beds, tidy their rooms, and prepare their meals. It stimulates those expensive tastes and habits that working-class university students also recognized they had acquired as part of their experience of higher education.

This generalized outcome of higher education is evident in the fact that, despite pedagogical differences in the methods of teaching and learning in different subjects of study at the three institutions, all interviewees estimated that they had acquired capabilities of a general and analytical kind, rather than specialized knowledge or particular technical skills, though very often these had been learnt as well. An ability "to see all sides of an argument" and "to solve problems" was felt to have been developed by nearly all students. Most of the students we spoke to felt that three or four years of full-time study had given them, if not an expertise, an overall familiarity with a given academic area, even if this was sometimes narrowly defined by traditional academic boundaries, and that the principles of understanding in their particular discipline were applicable in general terms to the intellectual comprehension of related and other areas. For example:

I think with physics you don't really change the way you think because it's a specialized area that you've already been introduced to and you just think, "how do the laws of physics apply and can what I know of maths apply to that?" I even do it when I'm watching telly.

Similarly,

the main skill of history is being able to take a large and incoherent body of information and put it into a coherent presentation, turning it into something understandable. I don't think it's a particularly tangible skill. I suppose by that I mean it's nothing directly employable.

Or, as another Home Counties student stated, "Really it's how to handle information rather than the information itself. "

In this sense, one Oxbridge interviewee could talk of the "training" that he felt his mind had received. This Newmanesque expression of the ideal of a liberal education is supposed to be uniquely developed by the Oxbridge tutorial system, extolled in the 1988 Oration of the

Vice Chancellor of Oxford as "the best method ever devised for training minds and exposing fallacies" (in Salter and Tapper 1992, 238). Nevertheless, it was an expression not used by the other interviewees, who were more likely to express this cognitive capacity that they felt they had acquired as a "general understanding" over "widened horizons", or as "logical" or "scientific thinking".

All groups of students agreed that it was mainly this cognitive, analytic or problem-solving capacity that had been developed as a result of their studies. Therefore, "the ability to learn how to learn" valued by the official pronouncements of employers and higher education administrators, or the "underpinning knowledge" necessary to supplement technical competence as measured, for instance, by the government sponsored general National Vocational Qualifications (NVQs), would seem to be the real acquisition of higher education in all three institutions (Jessup 1991).

This was particularly appreciated by Inner City students, in contrast with their previous experience:

> "I had such narrow views before [and] you think you know everything with just a little knowledge. [But now] nothing is cut and dried any more. Everything leads to a further question. I can never find an answer to anything. It's always "but", "what if?", "on the other hand". There's always more to find out. There's so many ways of looking at it. [So] you never take anything at face value any more [and become] more critical, detached, analytical, open-minded, leading to a broader view of the world [in which] I look at more issues now, objectively and from different points of view – a logical way of looking at things.

For Home Counties students, who echoed these views, this cognitive content was again "partly because you're getting older – you think more logically and don't, like, rush in so fast". But it was also much more than this, as expressed most cogently by the following students:

> I've come to understand more how the world around us is constructed ideologically rather than taken for granted . . . Nothing is the way it seems. Everything is constructed for some reason by some agency . . . I've got no particular interest in films; it just seems that's the only area where people have started to explore these ideas. You need to talk about something . . .

I'm quite transformed – sleepers awake – scales from the eyes, any cliché you like . . . I think differently, but it's very difficult to define. You can't unlearn something once you've learnt it. I read the papers differently and look at the government policy differently, and institutions – hospitals, police, schools, everything – a different viewpoint altogether. I realize things don't come down ready made. They're socially constructed. I also wish everybody could come and do it but there probably would be a revolution then. I don't think I would've thought like this when I was 18. Like Shaw said, education is wasted on the young.

This ability to talk and to think in a general, logical, rational or scientific way is clearly entangled with the cultural attitudes which Inner City students were also aware of acquiring, as illustrate by two brothers in conversation:

"You always have to doubt things . . . You want to know why . . ."
"To counter arguments before you say things . . . you become more, like, argumentative . . ."
"Well, more opinionated . . ."
"More objective . . ."
"Pessimistic . . ."
"Cynical."

The fact that this cultivation of the mind provided students with a leg-up the "hierarchy of credibility" was not lost on at least one Inner City student:

I've learnt the power of education and how you can exclude people and how as soon as you mention a degree you can shut a lot of people up and people will listen to you, 'cos in this job I have to deal with doctors to get prescriptions for people on heroin and so on. I mean, the last doctor I was dealing with, she asked me "Have you got the qualifications to do this job?" and I said, "Yeah, I've got a degree" and then she would talk to me like . . . And another thing it's taught me is that you can bullshit people with education, you can talk a lot of nonsense. It's power, you know. You can even make things up and they'll still believe you. There's a tremendous amount of power you know.

Working-class students at Home Counties also acquired what they saw as middle-class habits: "Like nice food and going to the opera and reading, which my parents would say was dead snobby", so that as another Home Counties interviewee added, whatever their class origins, students will "be middle-class by the time they leave here!"

> I mean, university changes you; you couldn't not change after three years in an elitist middle-class institution. I say "lunch" and "dinner" instead of "dinner" and "tea"! In a way I've come to accept it but that's the extent of it. I still find wine bars, like, obnoxious places. I don't think I've kind of taken on this middle-class kind of culture. That was something else that was alien to me. [For example] I'd been to a restaurant a couple of times in my life before I came here. Especially the first year when you don't want to miss out, I spent far too much money in restaurants . . . I've acquired this horrible middle-class habit of taking taxis and getting into debt – an overdraft, but it's all figures; it just doesn't mean that much. I remember I was extremely worried the first time I had, like, £200 overdrawn but now I don't worry. I've been given a £2,000 limit . . . . I still resent being called a snob because I've been to university. They think you must've been privileged to get there. The same thing as I faced from working-class kids on the council estate when I went into the sixth form.

Indeed, how far this cultural acquisition is distinct from what can be called a class ideology and how far it is formally taught as opposed to informally acquired is difficult to disentangle, if only because, as one Home Counties student stated:

> it's difficult to think back to before . . . it's hard to separate what you knew before from what you learnt. [So that] it's a loss of innocence really. Books were just books before. [Now] it's very hard to watch plays or read books without this other analysis going on in your head. [And] I think a lot differently. You sort of see things in a different light once you go into them.

Consequently, higher education had given students of working-class origins a choice. Like the heroine of *Educating Rita*, a mature Inner City student explained:

> You think differently and you speak differently without realizing it. You can go either way now. You can go with people like the people we used to go around with – you can come down to their level, but

you can also go up a level, to talk to people about their subject and understanding it.

In his classic formulation of the liberal idea of a university, Cardinal Newman declared that "not to know the relative disposition of things is the state of slaves and children (Newman 1943, 157) and, he could have added, of the majority of his working-class contemporaries in the mid-19th century.[4] In the 1990s, although it is possible for working-class people to acquire such an overall view and the same general cognitive abilities by their own efforts, without attending higher (or any kind of formal) education, it is normally acquired in conjunction with the acquisition of "badges of ability" which "certify" what Bourdieu has called marks of "distinction". Therefore, qualifications not only act as badges of ability and social distinction but also facilitate entry to "middle-class" society. At the same time, they inflict "symbolic violence" upon those who are excluded (Bourdieu 1986).[5]

The notion of studenthood as a cultural apprenticeship relates to the vexed question of students class of destination – whether, whatever their class of origin, the higher education process made them, as many interviewees stated, "middle class", although this was not a universal conclusion:

> Once you've got a degree you're sort of classified as a graduate and I think the influence or the impact of your social background sort of slides back, and the main thing is that you're a graduate, it's not so much you're middle, upper or working-class any more.

> I would definitely describe myself as working-class. I would describe most people as working-class. I think in today's understandings of class that we are being seduced into believing that class no longer exists. In my opinion the classless society does not exist. I have the impression that most people here are working-class, not that they might describe themselves like that, they might have been seduced by ego-problems into describing themselves as something else, not wanting to identify with the world of cloth caps and mufflers in todays world of designer dress. Established universities are mainly middle-class. There's not a lot of working-class access there at all. I don't really have experience of Oxford and Cambridge but I get the impression by their overt social behaviours that they act in ways that the working-class tend not to act in.

Well, I'd have to be realistic so I'd describe myself as middle class even if I didn't start off there, 'cos there's a thing called social mobility y'know, 'cos if you compared me to my parents we're not the same.

The lecturers say you're middle-class – we've discussed this endlessly in seminars but my background is working-class [parents both work on the line in a Midlands car factory]. I would like to be classless but everybody thinks about it so much I've got to the point where I think "I'm me" and that's it.

Social background? Ha! Now you touch on a very, very touchy subject there. Now then, I don't consider myself as part of the British class system. It all depends on what you use to classify social class. In terms of education you could say, "Yes, I am middle-class", right? Or my earning potential, if you like, but I don't think class stops there. I think you have to look at lifestyle, attitudes and culture. Now, I see myself first of all as an African woman. I can't identify with the traditional British middle class as such because I feel that my values and attitudes are very different because with class you've got to feel part of that group and I don't feel any identification with them nor with the working-class.

This question has been as widely debated by sociologists as, to judge from the responses of these interviewees, it apparently is by some of the students themselves, even though many of them, especially middle-class students from the established universities, eschewed any meaningful categorization of self or others in terms of social class. Answers given to this question by interviewees and by sociologists vary from the simple "by definition all students are middle-class" (mature Inner City student), to Erik Olin Wright's ambivalent neo-Marxist notion of statuses, such as those occupied by higher education students, having "contradictory class locations" in which individuals share attributes of the classes above and below them and from which they may transfer either upwards or downwards (Wright 1984).

The difficulty of classifying students by the usual occupational indices arises from the fact that students have no occupation as such, since most courses – save the most specifically vocational such as law, accountancy, medicine and architecture – do not relate to definite occupational outcomes but have general relevance to a range of jobs.

A student's occupation in the majority of cases is, therefore, as Bourdieu and Passeron (1964) remark, merely to prepare for an as yet unspecified occupation.

With the expansion of higher education and increasing divisions between graduates in the market for jobs the classification of students as a single "class" makes far less sense than it did at a time when the more highly educated constituted a select "elite" (Kelsall et al. 1972). A number of students were aware that social differentiation not only shaped the hierarchy of academic institutions, but also occurred among students in the same university. At Home Counties we were told:

> I mean you're still going to have your own groups, even when they come to university, I mean, you know, if you like to distinguish between upper, middle or working . . . three, . . . I don't like the distinction of three different classes [but] it's there, whether you like it or not, it exists . . . and some people feel it. But you do . . . they seem to stick in their own classes, their own groups, they feel safer, happier, I don't know . . . Just reinforces it . . . just continues it on to the next generation.

And at Inner City:

> There's a lot of middle class-students here who disguise themselves as working-class but don't really know what it means. There are very few upper-middle-class but you can spot them a mile away – they way that they talk, their views – they're very narrow minded. My sister is at [an established] university and it's amazing how differ-ent the range of people are. That's one thing that really struck me. They're very middle-class. The few working-class ones stick together. They're all the ones that are in the Socialist Party. That in-cludes my sister. I don't think she's one that's likely to conform!

Many of the students in this study had a clear idea of how their location in the academic hierarchy would affect their job chances. All students recognized that part of the selection process had *already* taken place. The university admissions procedures had, in the main, guaranteed the standard of the product because, as an Oxbridge student explained, "Obviously there are people who come to Ox-bridge interviews and are rejected just because their personality isn't rounded enough for entry; they don't seem open-minded enough".

So that, "It's more the fact that you've got into Oxbridge than anything you've done there that makes people think you've got something." And, as another added,

> I think it's traditional. I mean, it's been going back such a long time
> and if you talk to employers quite often they'll say they prefer an
> Oxbridge degree. I think the thing about their Oxbridge candidates
> is not that they're just good at their subject but they're all-rounders.
> I mean if they mention they've done drama they can virtually write
> the stuff. It's not just the subject, people are all-rounders, they're
> good in art and sciences or they can excel in extracurricular activi-
> ties. So I think that's the difference I found between Oxbridge and
> normal degrees.

The importance of the informal curriculum in developing such "all-
round" and work relevant skills was stressed even by this Oxbridge
interviewee, who conceded,

> OK, they don't know how to work a photocopying machine, they
> don't know how to work in an office, but they've been involved on
> committees for this, that and the other, they've directed shows, you
> know, a lot of things that you have the opportunity to do that I know
> you don't have the opportunity to do really when you go straight into
> a nine-to-five job.

In addition, as seen, "a common understanding with the people
around you" was valued by Oxbridge interviewees as a vital part of
their extracurricular student experience and this commonality of
experience clearly included employers also:

> I suppose that for a start a lot of people in top positions have come
> from Oxbridge.

> I think it's prejudice, not a nasty prejudice, but a belief that "we went
> through this so it's desirable and everybody else who we recruit,
> therefore, should have come through this".

> If you're targeting Oxford and Cambridge you are liable to reach a
> higher proportion of people who are trying to reach important
> careers . . . I think that's the basis for them recruiting from here. One
> of the theories behind that is that they like things that are similar;
> people don't generally try and get things which are dissimilar to
> themselves.

Many of our Oxbridge interviewees showed a clear awareness of employer demands. In fact, one had gone to the length of hiring a consultant to prepare his CV! This was the literary equivalent of being "presentable", "well-spoken", and showing "initiative" at job interviews. They also recognize a common cultural comprehension between Oxbridge students and ex-Oxbridge employers, formalized by the infamous "Old Boys Network", of which one Oxbridge student provided a classic instance:

> One example is if you are a [rugby] supporting blue you are able to join a university society called "The Hawks". Now I've got a friend who's a Hawk who went for an interview with a Hawks' tie on and the interviewer said, "Oh, is that a Hawks' tie?" and they then spent the next half-hour talking about golf clubs. He wasn't really clued up about the job and he wasn't really clued up about what he wanted to do or anything like that, and he ended up with the job.

The width of commonality could be narrowed to the shared experience of having attended the same Oxbridge college. "Certainly", as another interviewee opined, "the way merchant banking works, it's who you know, and there seems to be a lot of the old college network." So that, just as certain Oxbridge colleges maintain both formal and informal links, from bursaries and scholarships to regular contacts, for preferential recruitment from selected private schools, so some employers may narrow their first choice of recruit to particular Oxbridge colleges. In the case of certain law firms, for example, an Oxbridge law student felt "it is a distinct advantage to have been to one or two colleges in Oxbridge". Or at least to only one of two universities, so that "management consultancies, I would almost dare to say, they'd hardly bother anywhere else".

In this way, as Scott suggests,

> Without any need for a consciously intended bias in recruitment, the established "old boys" sponsor the recruitment through their networks of contacts of each new generation of old boys . . . The public schools and Oxbridge colleges are the foundations of these networks which interconnect the various upper circles . . . It is in and through the informal social networks which connect the upper circles that class reproduction is ensured. (1991, 117)

As a result, even though in terms of academic merit an Oxbridge degree was equal to any other higher education degree, in the realistic opinion of an Oxbridge interviewee, "BA Oxbridge means more than a BA somewhere else" because "in the market its value is greater". So that, "I think you start one step up the ladder by coming from Oxbridge."

Of course, such informal recruitment, as well as being class biased, works against any precise proportionality in the appointment of previously under-represented groups, such as ethnic minorities, women, or people with disabilities. Oxbridge interviewees were confused and divided on the issue of whether such discrimination existed – "ethnicitity [sic], I can't even say the word!", as one interviewee exclaimed – or, if it did, whether it applied more to gender than to race, or vice versa. The Oxbridge students can hardly be blamed for such confusion because, as some explained:

> There are relatively few coloured people here at Oxbridge still, really astonishingly few, particularly at the undergraduate level . . . In my college I think there's only two but they stick together and go to cafeterias together and . . . those people who do talk to them are very conscious of the fact that they're talking to blacks, as it were.

Typically, interviewees thought that the small numbers of black people at Oxbridge were because "I don't think that many will apply". The absence of students from ethnic minority backgrounds was also recognized at Home Counties:

> From being educated in a comprehensive, when I was at school it was largely with Afro-Caribbean and Asian pupils alongside me, probably they outnumbered white pupils. When I got to university the biggest shock of all was to see how under-represented at Home Counties we are with Afro-Caribbean pupils and by Asian pupils, I think I could count probably three or four that I've seen and they're very under-represented in this particular university. They're better represented in polytechnics, I know, because I've got friends at polytechnic and I think that's going to have an effect on how they fare in the labour market, because if they're going to be more highly concentrated in polytechnics then there's not going to be so much prestige attached when they go for interviews for jobs, whatever. I think, yes, they will be discriminated against.

Nevertheless, some interviewees (including a couple of women) considered that women and ethnic minorities were at an advantage when applying for jobs. For example:

> Nowadays it is extremely useful to be visible and to be slightly different, and I think if you came from a Oxbridge college background and you were black, but you were in all other respects assimilated [*sic*], then you would have a very strong advantage in going for a job.

The one male ethnic minority Oxbridge interviewee, a Kurdish mathematician going into advertising, considered that in that area "it's more on merit", although "it's mainly white males". This was, however, a minority view, especially among female students, for although they rarely expressed feelings of discrimination at university, many were aware that this might not be the case when they entered the labour market:

> I had an interview about a month ago and one of the interviewers said, "Now, I don't want to be sexist, but are you married or do you have a boyfriend?" and I mean it was a question he wouldn't have asked a guy. I think that it can work two ways. I mean, some companies want to improve their ratio and they think, "Yes, we'll maybe take the woman in preference because we don't think it's good having a totally male work force." There are other places who think that women are going to stop work to have children and they think they won't fit in properly and it's a long way down the corridor from the women's toilet or, you know, sort of, those kinds of attitudes. But I think it can work both ways. I think to some extent women are still at a disadvantage but hopefully it's changing.

> It depends on what job you're going into, but I know most people I've been asking and most girls I know have been asked about their family prospects and whether they're going to be popping off for a baby quite soon after they've got the job. I don't know how far, how much it influences employers, but it's a question that they ask a lot of people about.

Students from Home Counties and Inner City shared a cognitive map of the labour market with Oxbridge students at the apex:

> If you had an Oxbridge degree it means that you're quality, you've got that much . . . it's a status symbol in itself, it means, I suppose, you're good because otherwise they wouldn't accept you.

I envisage myself somewhere in an intermediate level because there's a certain . . . personality, a certain type of person that will fill a top notch position in a company, and that is not me . . . it goes beyond qualifications, it's who you know, it's your informal networks, who you meet, how good you are at your job which makes a difference, I think to a degree at that level, how cunning you are . . . how confident you are, your contacts as in family, if you've got good family contacts, if you've got good other business contacts, you know . . . Below that at the bottom, I've been at the bottom and I know what it's like at the bottom, and I think it truly is hell and what you're expected to do, what a days work involves, and I don't particularly want to be in that, so somewhere in the middle ground, whichever, whatever they want to offer me . . . it's difficult to tell.

These students were well aware of the advantages enjoyed in the labour market by their Oxbridge contemporaries. Whether or not they thought that they could overcome these disadvantage depended upon their labour market orientation towards the type of employment they sought after graduation. However, even if they did not seek top managerial and executive posts, or to pursue entrepreneurial careers in adaptive organizations, but aimed for the middle ranks of conventional, bureaucratic organizations, students from Home Counties and Inner City accepted that Oxbridge graduates would be preferred over them when applying for the same posts. In some cases they already knew this from their own experience at interviews. For example:

Well, the ones I've met during merchant banking interviews were definitely higher class. They all spoke with a potato in their throat and were all shocked when they heard I came from Home Counties not Durham or somewhere that would be a good second best to them . . . I have to be honest about it, they didn't like me; basically they said, "You went to the wrong university, my friend". Basically that's because Oxbridge people hire Oxbridge people.

Similarly, as an Inner City student observed:

I went for a job at a top property firm and they wanted to know, like, what your father does and what type of school you went to. They just want to know if you went to a public school or a comprehensive, state school. He didn't say, "What school did you go to?", he said, "What type of school did you go to?" . . . What irritates me in my course is, you know, I applied for the same jobs as some other people and I came top for three years and I know my "A" level grades weren't fantastic but I think they were the best on my course and when I applied for jobs the same as other people I never got a look in because the people who went to public schools, they got quite a few interviews and things, and, I mean, their grades over the three years, they were just average, like 50 per cent, and their "A" level grades were poor but they seemed to get more interviews. That's the facts.

In the same way, Oxbridge interviewees recognized that, save in the case of very specialized – and therefore also "limited" occupations requiring a particular degree perhaps from a new university, they would have advantages over non-Oxbridge applicants.

There is clearly little cultural commonality between students from families whose parents, and even grandparents, had attended university and sometimes even the same Oxbridge college and those at Inner City recruited from local state secondary schools and who were the first in their families to remain in education beyond 16 and then proceed to university (Jackson and Marsden 1966). One of the Inner City interviewees regarded students at Oxbridge as being so different from himself that they might well be "on another planet". However, the complaints from non-Oxbridge students did not focus on the existence of a system of occupational stratification with jobs highly differentiated according to pay and prestige, but on the fact that such rewards were allocated according to ascribed rather than more meritocratic criteria:

I would like to think that things like people from different ethnic backgrounds and sexes is being reduced, you know, the outlook of people . . . it doesn't matter what, whether they are male or female or what colour they are, if they can do the job they ought to get it, if they are the best person for the job . . . I don't know if it is in reality. I like to think it is . . . I think that if you are Oxbridge and you do humanities you are still given an unfair advantage merely on reputation, I feel that for both Oxford and Cambridge . . . I was told to apply to them, but then I refused to because of that . . . I feel that is wrong . . .

I think social background still makes a difference even though there are firms who are trying to say, well, you know, if you're a woman, well, even the firms with me, I suppose, I've got all the things against me, stacked against me, being black and a woman, and social background in the case of coming from a working-class as opposed to middle class, you know, does make a big contribution. I still think that plays a big part in particular jobs, in certain areas it may be broken down, but I think it will still take a while before social class or whatever doesn't really make a difference.

I went up to Cambridge last term and saw a friend in a bar and this was the eighth week and she hadn't been to class yet. I don't think you could get away with it here, frankly speaking. But you can get away with it in Oxbridge. I think people rely too much on reputation of the Oxbridge sect. I mean, obviously it is important, a lot of people say it is not what you know but who you know and when you leave you have sort of connections with the old boy network or the old girl network, or whatever it is, so if you want to get up and on after, say, five years in work, then, you know, it's a question of how fast you can get things done, who you know, and various internalized connections. I think there is a lot to be said for working hard on your own merits than getting a 2:1, it doesn't matter really where.

The BBC's very cliquey and I don't like that mentality at all. It's also . . . something like the Oxbridge mentality, where because there are a lot of Oxbridge people in the BBC, I think they can't help but be of that clique formation. If you are from Oxbridge you have a better chance of getting in and this sort of thing. It should be on merit.

At Home Counties University, although the students we interviewed were aware of changes in higher education, especially the rapid increase in student numbers, they were clear about where they stood in the hierarchy of IHEs. The fact that they were not part of the elite minority is sometimes through choice, when, as in two or three cases, they had rejected the offer of an Oxbridge place in favour of the degree programmes taught at Home Counties, or because: "I didn't want to get involved in that whole thing – the balls and the Boat Race". But more usually they have been relegated to what they realize is perceived as an institution of the second rank. Failure of admission to the elite universities is therefore rationalized by Home Counties "rejects" – as they sometimes referred to themselves or to some of their fellow students – by reference to illegitimate entry through social connections or in terms of the exceptionally "gifted" who gain acceptance by dint of their effortless achievement. Knowing that they are neither of these, some Home Counties students tend to play down their intellectual interests and to appear visibly indifferent to their courses of study. In such circumstances, the exhibition of "effortless achievement" can be deployed to fend off the accusation of "Oxbridge reject".

The exceptions here were the mature students and those from working-class backgrounds, or at least those who were among the first generation in their families to enter higher education. They were more likely to feel that they had been lucky or even privileged to have got so far. This accounts for their marked enthusiasm, in contrast to other students who largely take it for granted as part of what has become established within two generations (as a result of the first expansion of higher education in the 1960s) as a normal transition for middle-class youth from school to work and from home to living away (Jones and Wallace 1992).

There are, however, compensations from being in the second division of the academic hierarchy within what is still perceived by most as a privileged or fortunate student status. Students know that some subject choices are unique and some departments at Home Counties enjoy renown. They are also clearly aware of their superior position in relation to many other IHEs, and to the new universities in particular. Here university lecturers and tutors play a part in shaping student perceptions (Bourdieu 1988). At the same time, parental pressure in favour of established universities over what were previously polytechnics is also evident, and students are also more or less aware, depending upon their subject of study, of employer preferences for established university graduates:

> I think there's a lot attached to the sort of higher education you've been through, there's a difference in whether you've been to poly-technic and got a degree there, whether you've been to university of whether you've been to Oxbridge: there are distinct differences . . . To have a degree from university, I think it's got more prestige attached to it and more status than a degree from a polytechnic simply because if you go to apply then there are higher grades necessary for university and even higher grades required depend-ing on the area of the university – whether it is redbrick or whether

it's in a particular area: and then with Oxbridge, again, I think that's like the ultimate that you can achieve in higher education, is to go to Oxbridge and get a degree . . . I'm thinking [here] in terms of the labour market and sort of societal prestige and status, that that's the way the general public regard it. If I were to go to a job interview and I've gone to Oxbridge I'm sure I'd go down a lot better than me saying "Oh well, I went to Birmingham Poly or London Poly". I think with polytechnics people get the impression that you just sort of coasted through your "A" levels and just sort of got there and the polytechnic accepted you. To get to university I think you have to work a bit harder, there's a lot of status attached to getting straight "A"s or whatever and going to Oxbridge so I think the rewards in real terms are greater.

I've got to admit I tried for Oxbridge . . . I went there and hated the attitude of the place. You know, I didn't sort of question it really, the chance of getting there. I mean, I do generally feel I'm glad I didn't, but it's hard to say because I didn't get in and people feel I'm just saying that. I don't know whether it's justified or not these days getting into Oxbridge . . . It's a tradition, I suppose, I mean, probably the best people go there, so they want to get the pick of the best . . . I think in general, just knowing the reactions of my relations and family that have not been through any higher education, you know, grandparents and that generation, they'd definitely give a snob element that university is much better than polytechnic. I don't remember it being specifically said, but if you could get into university, you should. Polytechnic was considered somehow a second choice.

The immediate thing that springs to mind is, oh yeah, polytechnics are second-rate and universities are academic. I mean polytechnics are seen as training people for the workplace. I mean that was the whole, real object of polytechnics was a technical training . . . no matter how hard you try and think about it, in people's minds, I think also practically, there is a distinction between a university and a polytechnic, and universities are seen as higher academically . . . and therefore, certain snob appeal, and . . . you can't get away from that.

The students at Inner City University also had a clear perception of their position in the educational and consequent employment hierarchy. As one particularly despondent interviewee put it, "Let's face it, nobody comes to Inner City unless they're desperate!". Moreover,

> some students have gone to university on any course just 'cos it's a university, whereas they could've done things they wanted to do at a poly. At poly they haven't got that pressure. At the school I went to there was that pressure. All they cared about was the numbers they managed to get into Oxford and Cambridge. And from my parents – they were so disappointed when I went to a poly, not that it bothered me at all. Maybe university students do look down on poly students. Their grades were obviously better at "A" level that's all. If they went to university they obviously went to good schools, so in order to go to those schools their parents were probably from professional backgrounds but, saying that, I've got so many friends who've gone to university and they're not like that at all, so there might be a mixture as well. But it is the impression you get when you meet them. They tend to look down on you.

However, as with the Home Counties students in relation to the universities which they know are ranked above them, Inner City students appreciated that their degree courses are worth as much if not more, in terms of course content, as the same courses elsewhere. This was also emphasized to them by their lecturers, as one of them had told his students, "The polytechnics are the poor man's universities". The same lecturer also explained to his students that they would be expected to work harder for the same degree qualification because they had entered their course of study at a lower starting point – with relatively poor "A" levels, with other entry qualifications such as BTEC or City and Guilds, through "Access" programmes, or sometimes with no formal qualifications at all. However, they were told that their final degree qualifications would be of equal worth, even if the students knew that they would not be regarded as such by employers (Roizen and Jepson 1985). One interviewee explained the difference between established and new universities:

> I think there's a lot of snob value between poly and university. I think people would prefer to say they go to university than to polytechnic but I think that academically they're equal. It's a bit like grammar and comprehensive but you can get the same qualifications in both places.

Despite such self-assurances, the Inner City students picked up their perception of their place at the bottom of the hierarchy from their lecturers, from any comparison they are able to make with other university students on the same courses, and from the amount of work they are asked to undertake in order to reach the same level from a "lower" starting point. This estimation may well be reinforced by the changing of the names in the unified post-binary system, as well as by those shadows of the traditional university experience that percolate down to Inner City, which has recently redesignated it's largest site as a "campus", where new residential blocks are being built for the typical school-leaving student it now aims to attract. For these "mainstream" students, their experience of higher education at what is now Inner City University could become like that of students at Home Counties, with the same kinds of societies and social activities. Similarly, Home Counties University continues to imitate the cultural style, value and assumptions established by Oxford and Cambridge. But this will hardly be sufficient, we argue, to provide students with those indefinable and ambiguous "charismatic" qualities of "personal and transferable skills" demanded by employers for their organizations, modelled upon the "adaptive" paradigm. It is to the perceptions that students have towards their work and career prospects that we now turn.

Notes

1. Similarly within Oxbridge, women consistently achieve a lower proportion of first class and third class honours degrees (Davies and Hare 1989).
2. The full quotation from Simmel (1978) reads:

   Finally, I want to refer to the very characteristic fact that the accumulation of intellectual achievements, which gives a disproportionate and rapidly growing advantage to those who are favoured by it, also has its analogy in the accumulation of money capital. The structure of monetary relationships, the way in which money yields return and profits, is such that, beyond a certain amount, money multiplies without a corresponding effort on the part of the owner. This corresponds to the structure of knowledge in the cultural world which requires, beyond a certain point, decreasing self-acquisition on the part of the individual, because the cognitive content is increasingly offered in a condensed and, beyond a certain level, concentrated form. The highest stages of education require less effort for every step further than the lower stages, and yet at the same time produce greater results. Just as the objectivity of money permits "work" that is ultimately relatively independent of personal energies and the accumulating returns lead automatically to more accumulation in growing proportions, so the objectification of knowledge, the separation of the results of intelligence from its process, causes these results to accumulate in the form of concentrated abstractions, so that, if only one stands high enough, they may be picked like fruits that have ripened without any effort on our part. (p. 442)

3. The idea of effortless achievement which harbours notions of natural gifts and social grace

supplies the privileged classes with a legitimation of their cultural privileges, which are thereby transmuted from a social heritage into individual grace or personal merit. Behind this mask "class racism" can be flaunted without ever being seen for what it is. This alchemy succeeds all the better inasmuch as, far from challenging it with an alternative image of scholastic success, the working-classes take over the essentialism of the upper classes and experience their disadvantage as a personal destiny. (Bourdieu and Passeron 1964, pp. 69-70)

4. Such cultural knowledge is distinct from, but common to, what the evaluator of the Enterprise in Higher Education Initiative at Inner City noted are "the distinct cultures of different courses" that are "a product of admissions procedures, staff attitudes, and, crucially, the intrinsic, cognitive status of curriculum content", by which "the dispositions of individual applicants, curriculum content, and institutional ethos are moulded together to constitute a marketable commodity". This insight relates not only to the differences between students of different subjects, especially arts and science students, but also to those between institutions, following as it does Bourdieu's previous description of the French *grandes écoles* objectively located in a structural map on the basis of the self-constructions which they had effected in their selection procedures" (in Robbins 1991, 166).

Despite the constant shifts and realignments of the status hierarchy of subjects of study within and across institutions, the same differentiation is observable between low status, technical and vocationally applied subjects that are closely taught through rigidly structured programmes, as against high status, theoretical, pure and non-vocationally applied subjects acquired through a largely self-directed, informal cultural apprenticeship in the discipline. Cross-cutting this general principle of differentiation, however, is that of gender, which tends to lower the status of subjects that attract majority female students and staff, and the same could be said on a smaller scale for that of race.

5. Moreover, Pierre Bourdieu has pointed out how culturally arbitrary qualifications can change their worth as badges of distinction acquired by different social groups and how new signs of exclusion can be elaborated by elites to preserve privileged access to powerful positions. This process is being accelerated today (see Robbins 1991). Bourdieu developed what he called "a general anthropology of power and legitimacy" that helps to explain the system of cultural differences between groups and individuals developed from the past by modern consumer capitalism. It is an important principle of his explanation that the marks of social classification inflict "symbolic violence" upon those who are unable to acquire the "cultural capital" needed to maintain or advance their position from the base of the social hierarchy. As Bourdieu also indicated, the signs of cultural distinction are arbitrary and constantly altered by those in a position to control the rules of the game, such as the arbiters of taste and fashion, or the "Homo Academicus" who set the constantly varying entry criteria for higher education (Bourdieu 1988).

At the same time, individuals and groups, especially young people asserting an adult status in the existing hierarchy for the first time, also construct their own identities (in what Bourdieu calls their "life space" or "habitus"), using such resources as are available to them, either to conform to or diverge from the predominant norms presented to them. In this situation, as Bourdieu (1992) has written recently of the French schools:

> the official diversification (in grading) or the officious diversification (in institutions . . .) also has the effect of helping to create a principle of differentiation which has been meticulously concealed: the well-born pupils who have received from their families a well-honed sense of their position and, additionally, examples of advice capable of sustaining them in the event of uncertainty, are in the process of placing their [cultural] investments at the right moment and in the right place, that is to say, in the right career streams, the right establishments and the right departments. In contrast, those from the most disadvantaged families . . . are forced to be reconciled to the school's injunctions or to chance to find their way through a more and more complex universe and are, therefore, bound to invest at the wrong time and in the wrong way a cultural capital which is, in any case, extremely limited.

This is one of the mechanisms which, added to the logic of the transmission of cultural capital, ensures that the highest educational institutions, especially those leading to positions of economic and political power, remain as exclusive as in the past. This is the way that this system of education, which is widely available to all and yet plainly reserved for the few, pulls off the *tour de force* of bringing together the appearance of "democratization" and the reality of reproduction accomplished with a greater degree of deception and, therefore, with an increased effect of social legitimation.

CHAPTER FIVE

Student orientations to work and careers

In this chapter we consider the orientations to work of the students that we interviewed in our three participating universities. In our interviews, we were particularly concerned to determine how far our respondents were aware of the ways large-scale organizations were restructuring, and the implications this would have for their own employment prospects. Would they continue to subscribe to traditional notions of career progression, or were they developing conceptions of the labour market that would encourage them to develop more innovative and flexible employment strategies? In our opinion, either was possible in view of the impact of broader ideological and institutional changes on the one hand, and factors shaping personal experience and hence their expectations, on the other.

In view of the former, it could be that students are becoming increasingly aware of the decline of traditional bureaucratic forms of organization, and associated with this, the ending of career routes whereby managerial, professional and technical employees are able to enjoy incremental and status rewards within the relative shelter of clearly defined corporate structures. There are a number of forces that could be enhancing students' awareness of this. Probably one of the more important of these is the home background of the majority of our students, especially at Home Counties and Oxbridge Universities. With a parent or parents in managerial, professional and various kinds of white-collar occupations, in both the public and private sectors, they are likely to become increasingly knowledgeable about the direction of organizational change. More particularly, they may become aware that such changes are destroying the stability and relative security of traditionally defined middle-class occupations. During the late 1980s and early 1990s, their parents have been particularly vulnerable to corporate "down-sizing" as organizations have been forced to become "leaner", "slimmer" and "fitter" in order to be more competitive and cost-effective. The application of performance indicators to managerial work, the widespread implementation of information technology, and the imposition of ever-tighter budgets in order to reduce costs (especially in public sector organizations) has led to a rapid increase in the level of unemployment among white-collar and managerial employees as well as creating job insecurities for those remaining. It would be hardly surprising, then, if students in their home lives did not become more aware of these processes, and that they re-adjust their work orientations and career aspirations accordingly. Indeed, this could be reinforced by the "feedback" they obtain from friends and other acquaintances who have already experienced firsthand the extent to which employers are no longer able to offer long-term career prospects of the sort to which university graduates are traditionally accustomed (Boys et al. 1988).

Alongside such immediate experiences, however, there is also a major ideological force that could be shaping student aspirations. Since the early 1980s we have witnessed the growth of "entrepreneurship" and the increasing popularity of entrepreneurial ideals in the market economies of Europe and the United States (Gamble 1988, Krieger 1986). Britain has not been exempt from these, and whether or not "Thatcherism" was a cause or effect of such ideals remains an issue of debate (Hall and Jacques 1989). But certainly, the political culture of Britain changed in the 1980s and within this context, classical entrepreneurial values associated with enterprise, self-reliance and rugged individualism were offered, and continue to be offered, as the solution to the nation's difficulties, and particularly to the economic recessions that have been a recurrent feature of Britain in the 1980s and early 1990s (Overbeek 1990). Within this ideological rhetoric, the large-scale organization has been generally discredited, if only for the fact that it inhibits risk-taking. One of the major objectives of the industrial policies pursued by Conservative administrations for more than a decade has been to dismantle the bureaucratic cultures and structures of both public and private sector organizations. Hand in hand with this process has been the implementation of policies that encourage corporations to "de-collectivize" the employment relationship and in its place to offer individual, fixed-term contracts in addition to performance-related payment systems and various share-option and profit-sharing schemes for senior employees. Thus, within this "Brave New World", there is little place for security, long-term employment prospects and age-related payment systems (Handy 1989).

Moreover, the appeals of the politically-driven entrepreneurial culture have encouraged people to set up their own businesses (Curran and Blackburn 1991). Self-employment and small business start-up have been offered as a solution to long-term unemployment and as a means whereby innovation and creativity within all economic spheres can be revitalized. Within these appeals, the aspirations of university graduates have not been neglected. In the late 1980s the Graduate Enterprise Scheme was established, soon to be followed by the Higher Education Enterprise Initiative (Brown and Turbin 1989). The former was explicitly geared to developing the specific skills required for business start-up, while the latter was orientated towards changing the more general psychological predispositions of university students. Taken together, the intention has been to encourage graduates to be more independent and self-reliant and to pursue working lives that are not protected by the shelter of the large bureaucratic organization. Instead, students have been encouraged to expect uncertainty and change in their employment, and to view rewards as a return for innovation and effort rather than relating only to age and experience.

But how far have these broader ideological changes affected the attitudes of students? We ask this since there are a number of other factors which may be considered to be inhibiting, such as psychological reorientation. Perhaps one of the more implicit of these is the nature of the educational process itself which students have experienced since the beginning of their compulsory schooling. Although there have been explicit attempts to introduce more entrepreneurial perspectives, not only among university students but also among pupils within the school system (Dale et al. 1990), the reality for the majority is that schools and universities continue to operate according to bureaucratic principles. Notwithstanding the relative day-to-day "looseness" of university settings within which students are able to enjoy a high degree of personal autonomy – certainly by comparison with those in employment – most institutions of higher education are structured according to clearly-defined procedures whereby the academic staff are perceived by students as enjoying relative employment security and life-long career prospects.[1] With these persisting rôle models, students are taught and examined according to bureaucratic procedures which have changed little in the established universities over decades. Hence, despite explicit attempts to change student attitudes through such programmes as the Higher Education Enterprise Initiative, the day-to-day experiences of the majority of students are those which, at least until recently, offered an organizational "reality" of structure and security. It would hardly be surprising, then, if students did *not* generalize from these immediate experiences to their own future career prospects.

Clearly, there are a variety of experiences that will shape student orientations to the labour market. In order to explore the character of these it is possible to identify analytically "clusters" of attitudes which can be described as "conformist" and "non-conformist" but which, in turn, can be further disaggregated into a number of more refined subcategories. We label as *conformist* those who are committed to pursuing occupational careers as central to their own personal development. Conversely, those with a *non-conformists* orientation reject the notion of an occupational career as being central to their personal identities; in other words, a career is marginal to their life interests.

Among the conformist orientations, there are those who can be seen as subscribing to a *traditional bureaucratic* view. We would expect such students to have only limited awareness of the ways in which organizations are restructuring and the implications of these for their own future work patterns. They would perceive work as a career which can be pursued within the context of a single organization. For them, employment will consist of an orderly progression between jobs within a clearly-defined organizational hierarchy. Accordingly, they would feel able to plan their futures, including their personal lives, with reference to the traditional organizational principles of promotion and age-related salary incrementation.

Such a perspective is in sharp contrast to an alternative conformist orientation which we describe as *flexible*. We would expect such students to be knowledgeable about the ways in which modern organizations are restructuring and the broader effects of these for labour market participation. They recognize the declining availability of traditional bureaucratic careers and acknowledge the need to be both adaptive and mobile within the occupational sphere. Hence, they would perceive their futures as consisting of the need to move within and between organizations in frequent and unpredictable ways. Such students are likely to have *instrumental* perceptions of any future employers, since they perceive any corporate appointments as likely to be short-term and temporary. Accordingly, they would view their futures as consisting of constant change and uncertainty with the need to acquire flexible, transferable work-related skills, as part and parcel of compiling a coherent and "planned" work portfolio.

A more exaggerated expression of this desire to avoid corporate dependency is likely to be found among those students who could be described as holding an *entrepreneurial* orientation toward the occupational order. Although, by comparison with the "traditional bureaucratic" and the "flexible" approaches, such students would be expected to have internalized the ideological messages and the political rhetoric of the past decade. They would be inclined to be adverse to working for large organizations, but at the same time they are more likely to be highly committed to notions of personal and material success. Equally, they would emphasize the importance of obtaining self-fulfilment and personal development within work. As a result, these students are attracted to entrepreneurship and self-employment. They may recognize the need to work for large organizations in order to obtain work experience, but in the longer term their aspirations will be to manage their own businesses. Such students are more likely to be aware of the availability of various non-curricular entrepreneurial ventures while at university.

If, then, it is possible to determine three analytical subcategories of conformist orientations, a number of various non-conformist perspectives can be conceptualized. The first of these can be described as the *drop-out* orientation. Such students will have little or no intention of either pursuing careers in large organizations or of starting their own businesses. Instead, their orientations will be geared towards cultivating alternative lifestyles. In many ways, they will be the contemporary equivalents of the hippy generation of the 1960s, given that they are neither committed to the established industrial order nor to its predominant values. If they give any thought to employment and the occupational order, it is in terms of a *marginal* attachment. Essentially, they look for jobs that will give them sufficient income to "get by". These tend to be of a highly temporary and low skilled nature – working in pubs, restaurants, wine bars, etc. – and certainly they have no conception of life-long careers through which upward mobility can be expressed via job incrementation. After graduation, we would expect some of these students to reappraise their world views and to develop less negative attitudes towards the occupational order. Indeed, some are likely to develop views similar to those of another of our conceptual categories, the *ritualists*.

The ritualists recognize the need for employment but they define this solely in relation to the need for income. For them, work will not offer a channel for self-development and personal enrichment. Careers are unimportant, since the pursuit of them would require the investment of psychological and emotional inputs which they are not prepared to make. Instead, work is perceived as being a "necessary evil", something that has to be endured in order to underwrite a satisfactory, albeit modest, standard of living. Such students will, therefore, be attracted to jobs which they perceive to require the minimum of psychological investment to obtain necessary financial rewards. Paradoxically, they are inclined to seek employment within bureaucratic organizations, since their hierarchical structures, rules, clarity of procedures and relatively precise job descriptions offer psychological shelter, order and comfort. In this way they are able to maintain a psychological distance from their jobs and to rôle-play, thereby preserving the capacity to develop central life interests and personal identities *outside* rather than *within* work. We would expect such students to give priority to personal relationships over material success. Equally, leisure and cultural interests will be seen to offer alternative channels for self-enrichment and life satisfaction. For many, their university studies will provide the basis for the longer-term cultivation of artistic, intellectual and cultural interests of one kind or another, while others will be attracted to ideals of community involvement. In these ways, then, employment is regarded solely as a means whereby such interests can be materially underwritten.

In many ways, the orientations of these students will have many similarities with those of our final category, the *socially committed*, who will place their concern for various ideals before their own occupational careers and material self-interest. Students with this orientation are often reluctant to seek employment in profit-making corporations and limit their choices to public sector, charitable organizations and different kinds of pressure groups. For example, there are those who wish to improve the quality of the environment and others who are committed to the needs of the disadvantaged and various minority groups. For such students, career progression and material rewards will be of little importance and instead, they search for personal satisfaction through working in jobs which they consider to be socially responsible. Through this means, they reject the conformist values and assumptions found among those who have orientations which we have described as "bureaucratic", "flexible" and "entrepreneurial".

Clearly, such conceptual categories are not mutually exclusive, and neither are they "fixed" or "static", given that we would expect students to have relatively complex world views, which are subject to change with life experience. As a result of their direct participation in the labour market, for instance, if earlier expectations remain unfulfilled they are likely to redefine their work aspirations.[2] How many graduates entering the teaching profession, for example, become disappointed because they feel that they are unable to "educate" the young? How many of those joining environmental organizations become frustrated through feeling they are unable to bring about fundamental change? Equally, how many graduates join business organizations, but feel unable to express their ideas or develop their talents? Even so, such a conceptual categorization of student orientations is useful, since it offers an interpretive framework for analysing our data. Indeed, it is clear that student perspectives are *not* randomly determined but are a consequence of systematic differences in their material circumstances as shaped by such factors as social class, race, gender and educational biography.

The defining feature of the "conformist" category is a commitment to an occupational career. For these students, who accounted for the vast majority in our study, work was seen as being vital to their personal development, although there were significant variations in the weight given to an occupational career when set against other considerations, such as "having a good social life", "having a family", "doing something that interests me", "something which is of benefit to others".

I think you've got to find a job that you are going to be suited to, that you're going to get satisfaction from, because ultimately it's going to be central to your life, to your friends, the way you behave, the way you act, the way you dress. I think it's important that you find a rewarding job, not just financially but in terms of social life, whatever, so that's what I'm looking for, a job that I can find satisfaction and economic rewards, and also the opportunity as you say to carry on getting professional qualifications, training, so you can see some sort of pattern, some sort of mobility, so you can see yourself, where you're working towards rather than just entering a company at a particular level and wanting to stop there. I think people like to see where they're going to, where they could be going to, something to work towards, rather than expecting to remain in the same position.

I'd say a career is important, even if it's just in terms of your own independence, you know, doing what you want. I would prefer to be in a job that has some sort of activity in it than what people call a dead-end job, so I think a career for me would be important.

I don't think power and status are important. I wouldn't want to stay on the bottom rung of things [although] it's not desperately important for me to get to the top, I'm really not that keen on being in a situation where basically you're having to stand on other people's shoulders, you know, scramble to the top, but I'd hope to make a good job of what I was doing and be rewarded for it . . . I would go and do my best and see where I went to. It is important because I wouldn't want to just be doing a job that wasn't interesting. Obviously one's got to work to get money somehow and I'd prefer to do that in an interesting way.

The largest category of conformist students were those who subscribed to a "traditional bureaucratic" world view and who framed their occupational futures in terms of making a long term commitment to an organization, which in turn would provide incremental career progression. The traditional bureaucratic career is premised on regular and predictable increases in salary, status and responsibility as they climb the organizational hierarchy. The challenge for these students was to make something of themselves within the organization, rather than through the development of a labour market portfolio involving regular job changing or through self-employment.

A career structure is important. I've always had a structure. I've always known what I was doing next, like in my career in nursing. I see this job as part of that; the nursing has helped me get the job and it helps me in the job as well . . . I see it as a ladder. That's how I see my working life, as a ladder. You don't necessarily climb it at each stage, sometimes you move sideways to collect more experience before you go on up the next rung. That's what I've done at Inner City really, to get knowledge to take with me to the next stage. I wouldn't see a career development as something where you just jump to the top without the knowledge and experience. I think that's very important.

Once I'm in there I can always progress. I might apply to a chartered accountants but I'll see . . . Whatever I go into I'll move up the ladder . . . but I don't get a career until I've moved into management and then I see myself working my way up . . .

I'll stick at some place that I'm reasonably happy with, and I'll try and work my way through, get to know the ropes and things, rather than move around. I mean, for a start it's not my kind of competitive instinct to try and keep moving like that, it's not me . . . If I can work my way up, not under too much pressure, then I'll take those opportunities that come . . .

I think the biggest thing you have to do is enjoy the job, look, look forward to it, job satisfaction, looking forward to promotion, you can be, in the army, you can be guaranteed if you do your exams properly (looks like I'll be doing exams for the rest of my life) you can be assured of making captaincy by 28, 29. My father was made up to Colonel, a Lieutenant Colonel from a Private, which is almost unheard of these days, and I'd like to go at least a grade higher than him.

This traditional bureaucratic orientation harboured an assumed correspondence between their academic and occupational careers. It is assumed that they will find their place in the organizational hierarchy according to the exercise of technical expertise and "objective knowledge" and the service they provide, "rather than the possession or lack of inherited wealth or acquired capital" (Perkin 1989, 395), in much the same way that student careers involve regular examination of objective achievement. Here, then, the route to a successful occupational career is seen to be achieved through access to privileged knowledge (accredited by professional bodies) and the display of bureaucratic competence in the exercise of one's official duties, assessed according to formal meritocratic standards.

This orientation was particularly common among those who hoped to enter the established and quasi-professions; that is, as civil servants, schoolteachers, accountants, and so on. Their future employment was seen as providing "respectability" rather than "glittering prizes", although many of the students in this category were ambitious to obtain senior posts during the course of their careers. Moreover, a traditional bureaucratic career was seen to offer a predictable path into "professional" middle-class society. This was particularly important for those students from working-class backgrounds, ethnic minorities, and a large proportion of women. For them, the existence of formal career structures and job security was seen to be of particular importance, given their "social" marginality. This was generated by upward mobility within the educational system which had led to feelings of social isolation because of their detachment from their working-class social origins and "insecure" integration within the middle class. [3] For working-class students, who were among the first generation in their families to enter higher education, a traditional bureaucratic orientation was designed to secure occupational mobility.

Most of the Asian and Afro-Caribbean students were also in this category because they believed that traditional bureaucratic careers provided shelter from discrimination in competition for jobs:

> Being in a stable, secure job where one's ability is recognized and the chances of promotion are there. There's more to it as well . . . I think maybe the fact that I'm a black male might actually enhance my chances in certain jobs because I know for a fact that some boroughs are crying out for black social workers, and the probation service as well. Besides which I'm the right age. I've got experience of life and experience of working as a social worker, so all these are plus factors.

Moreover, two Asian engineering students who had found employment as local government engineers, which, if not so well-paid as the private sector, was regarded as being more secure and accessible to them. The question of discriminatory factors which may create barriers in the development of a career was also recognized by a number of female students in this category. Nevertheless, the traditional bureaucratic route was recognized to offer a solution to the career–family conflicts for many of the female students in this study.

> I would like to have children, but then you've got considerations . . .

if, for instance, I withdrew from my career to have children, wanted to spend time with my children as they grew up, then that's going to impair my progress, my sort of promotion within a company, and they're going to look at it like that. When they interview a female graduate, they say to you, are you getting married, have you got a boyfriend, not so directly but that's what they mean. If you say to them you're engaged or you've got a boyfriend, then they're wary of that, they do want women that are going to be prepared to build up a career, and I think as soon as you start thinking about children (which ultimately I would do) you have to look at it in a light of, how's that going to affect my lifestyle, my standard of living, economic situation . . . and you start weighting things up . . . I would like to have children, I think it would be very wrong to sacrifice having children just to have a career . . . because there are things in life which you know, you should experience. You know they haven't got any economic reward attached to them or any social status, but they're things all the same that should be valuable to you as a person. I think that you, you'd be forced into a situation where you're going to have to balance off that personal value of wanting children, that sort of fulfilment against the economic social rewards.

Although the vast majority of female students want to enter an occupational career on leaving university, many anticipated this as a potential problem and recognized that the interruption in their professional lives which child rearing inevitably entailed was more manageable in organizations offering a traditional bureaucratic career structure. This was especially where they saw themselves as being able to depart from employment for future child rearing and then return, if only part-time, in the classic female pattern (Crompton and Sanderson 1990):

"Once I've become a chartered accountant it's a good qualification which they can't take away from you, so if I were to take a break to have a family or something I could come back into it." Unlike many of the other female students, she expected her partner to organize his career in exactly the same way so that he could play an equal part in child care. Others were less sanguine, as a woman graduate admitted, "realistically" she would be "the one to stay at home and look after the children", and another, "Whoops, there goes my feminism out of the window!". Nevertheless, both male and female students in this category anticipated that their future partners would be free to pursue their own careers rather than seeing them as subordinate to their own. Hence, despite the hierarchical authority relations they recognize in bureaucratic organizations, in their private lives they seek open, expressive and egalitarian relationships:

> I don't, I don't think I could ever live my life just being a sort of support for a husband or for a partner. I don't think I could . . . handle having a partner who was very successful, whatever, and me to just be in the background supporting him, sort of . . . backing him up. I wouldn't be able to deal with that, I'd like to . . . be on an equal, equal footing . . . I think I can be quite . . . dominating at the best of times: I wouldn't be able to handle the sort of 'what' second best, Oh well, you're earning the most and your job is really important and I'm not, I'm just there to help you, I wouldn't be able to cope with that, I'd have to have something of my own . . . that was of importance to me. I would like to have somebody to share it with me and I would like to share their interest, their career, but I wouldn't be able to sort of give myself to somebody else's career, and say, well the meaning of my life is to help somebody else. It would have to be like . . . sharing each other's, helping each other, it couldn't be being dependent.

The high priority given to job security by all these students in no way implied that they expected their future jobs to be boring. Almost without exception, they anticipated entering traditional bureaucratic careers which would be satisfying, challenging and enjoyable:

> At certain stages I would review it [my career] . . . if I really was not enjoying it then I would leave, but, you know, I wouldn't just leave for the sake of it. I'd give it serious, careful consideration because by that stage, you know, late twenties, I will hopefully have other responsibilities as well, you know, family, mortgage sort of things, so I don't really want to . . . really at that stage, want to shift . . . If I was getting no job satisfaction, even if I had security, I would think about moving, but I imagine you have to weigh the two things.

Again, this was particularly noticeable from the responses of mature working-class students from both Home Counties and Inner City who had previously experienced the realities of semi-skilled or unskilled labour in factories or offices. The idea of getting a "job with prospects" was one of the main reasons for going to university. But this was frequently combined with a commitment to the "service ideal" of the established professions (Larson 1977, Perkin 1989), a sense of serving clients and society, with a detachment and an absence of self-interest which might influence their actions and advice.[4]

A growing number of these students were worried by "privatization" in the public sector and a growing awareness of organizational changes in the private sector, although at this stage in their career the overriding concern was that of finding an appropriate job irrespective of what this would subsequently involve. The security of the professions, and indeed their very claims to professional status (whether in terms of access to privileged knowledge or self-regulation), have been increasingly undermined of late, especially in the public sector. Interviewees were aware of these tendencies towards flexibility and insecurity and these were universally deplored by conventionally career-minded students, especially where parents, if teachers, doctors or civil servants, had been involved in the process. For most of these students it was the privatization of the health service and education which was the focus for their objections, primarily based on the fact that it undermined the ideal of a public service. In general, the importation of a cash nexus into areas of public service was seen as detracting from the essential interests and rewards that the students hoped to gain from their occupational careers. For example:

> I want to feel that I'm doing something that is important and making money for some multinational company is not something I feel is important. I want to do something that even in a small way will actually change things. I don't know though, it's really horrifying when everything's so cash-constrained in the real world; I don't know if it's possible to do these things anymore. I could have left school and got quite a well-paid job but I stayed on and went to university and everything because I wanted something self-fulfilling.

Those students with a traditional bureaucratic orientation who were looking for jobs in the private sector were equally aware that the adaptive firm could mean that it is "easier for them to get rid of you basically". This particular Home Counties student, sponsored through his course in computer systems engineering by a large company, was not alone in recognizing that job security was under threat, given that a bureaucratic career depended above all on an extensive occupational

98

hierarchy and job security. Without these, such students would not be able to realize a return on their investment of time, energy and skills.

The second-largest category of students in our study held "flexible" orientations to future employment. Occupational careers were perceived in terms of frequent job changes in the construction of incremental career portfolios rather than through progression within bureaucratic hierarchies. However, there is little that is arbitrary about their employment decisions, since they are dedicated to constantly adding value to their curriculum vitae, in terms of gaining professional qualifications and high-status work experience through appointments with the "right" companies:

> I would like to get a job and get to learn as much as I could about that particular company, about the way it operates, and then hopefully go to another company. I don't think it would be wise to look at a job for life. As a graduate I don't think you should leave university at the age of 20-21 and say I'm going to join this company and hopefully spend the rest of my life with it. I think there's a lot of benefit and gain in being mobile, both geographically and between different companies, because that's the way you're going to learn about how companies operate differently around the country, you know, abroad if possible. I think it's good for you to see how different companies operate. I might have this job for the rest of my life, for 40 or 50 years, it's too much of a commitment to make.

> A career was important at the time when I was doing nursing but then, since I've been on to study, I think things change, so, as for going up the ladder in the probation service, I really don't see myself going up the ladder because I don't think I want to stay there. It's like a means to an end for me, to get experience. I enjoy what I'm doing but in the long term I don't see myself becoming a Chief Probation Officer, or whatever, but you never know, circumstances in life change, but at the moment I see myself more branching out into something else because also, as you find out more about the work, you find out about different things and you think, "Oh, I didn't know about that", so perhaps I might find something more appealing and, also, with everything changing in the probation service, the ideas that I came into the service with, that all might change, so it's difficult to say where I will end up.

To all intents and purposes they shared many of the same goals as students exhibiting a traditional bureaucratic orientation. They want a "challenge", job satisfaction, social status, and material rewards befitting a professional person. They believed that they would be contributing to the good of society, although this was usually seen to come from improvements in company performance and customer satisfaction, rather than through working in the public sector. They also shared a belief that they needed to develop the capacity to be self-reliant and to avoid corporate dependency. In their view, provided they make the necessary effort, they can make a success of their "careers", as illustrated by this student about to enter accountancy:

> Initially I'll be a dogsbody – that's standard. But . . . It's a good training leading to a flexible qualification . . . and the organization I've joined is very much meritocratic and open, so hopefully after a year I'll be minding my own small team on an audit and thereafter you progress quite rapidly . . . The main problem is the professional examination. It's very hard to do but in the organization I'm going to about 80 per cent pass. The work itself I'm not worried about . . . If they feel I'm doing well in a certain area they will advance me and give me the pay increases, etc., as they see fit and that is important to me. I'll specify my own objectives within agreed organizational objectives with a counselling senior manager. That strikes me as an open and innovative idea . . . or I'll transfer to another sector within the organization but after six years about 60 per cent of people who go in for accountancy transfer out to industry. You basically write your own cheque and go where you want . . . I'm not looking for security . . . I need to be in a job where I've got authority.

In so far as they shared the same material ends, the means by which the "traditional bureaucratic" and "flexible" students intended to reach their goals were entirely different. Students with flexible orientations welcomed the new possibilities that they saw emerging as a result of corporate restructuring and the rhetoric of the enterprise culture. Rather than seeing the restructuring of bureaucratic organizations as a threat to job security they were seen as a challenge and opportunity to exercise initiative and show one's worth. Indeed, many of the aspects which were associated with traditional bureaucratic carers were eschewed by these students. An Oxbridge student who had been on work experience in a multinational computer company felt that in "such a large company, it's almost impossible to be anything more than a cog in the works".

This was a disposition reinforced by another male student on work experience, again from Oxbridge University: "Working for a large industrial company put me off engineering literally . . . It's just like generally running things and organization of menial tasks . . . It's a lot of effort and not much reward, basically." A challenging occupational career was described by another Oxbridge student studying Biology and Management Studies, who had got a job with a City firm of management consultants as:

> a job that wouldn't bore me, that would involve not sitting in the same office doing the same thing again and again, so with consultancy each time you have to move in, absorb and try to understand something in a very complex situation very quickly, which I think is a real challenge, and to understand the real problem that is going on to reach a solution, sort of analysing the situation to see what is going on, and again it's a changing environment. It's very dynamic stuff . . . I just don't see myself staying in one job my whole life.

Therefore, instead of seeking steady incremental progress within the same organization, the students in this category exhibit an impatience with the routine and time-serving aspects of conventional careers. For those with a flexible orientation the end-game was, as these Home Counties students explained:

> Jumping up horizontally, going from one company to another, gaining experience and perhaps coming back to the first company at a much higher level.

> I've got it planned out: the first three years for professional qualification doing auditing and business advisory to a wide range of clients. Post-qualification – a secondment of about six months to two years abroad, preferably France. The firm I'm joining encourages this because the main office is now in Europe. Then after that a couple of years in insolvency work and then after about five to ten years I want to move out into management consultancy. Beyond that the only problem is I don't know all the options that are going to present themselves, so I'll either go one of two ways – either break away and start my own business or climb as high as I can up the career ladder, or in industry try to become managing director of

Shell and become Vice-Chancellor of Home Counties University! Ultimately a managing director or chairman of a company, whether on my own or where I've got up through merit.

The *raison d'être* of this orientation is to short-circuit the corporate hierarchy. It is seen as a way of making rapid progress towards senior managerial and executive positions, without being locked into a bureaucratic career structure. A feature of this orientation was a reluctance to make a longer-term commitment to any organization, which in the industrial sector meant that:

> Industry is still, I'm afraid, regarded as being the lesser . . . I think there is still a feeling against it and an element of maybe snobbery against the idea of leaving university and going in at the low level of industry and fighting your way up . . . Having said that, though, there is definitely a route which goes management consultancy, two years business school, two years back to management consultancy, and then two years going into industry at the top end.

Management consultancy embodied the flexible orientation, although other jobs in the City, law and accountancy were also popular. A number of students seeking employment in biotechnology, electronic engineering and information technology also shared this orientation, where the immediate concern was to gain the relevant progressional qualifications to build their career portfolios. This was also the case among those who sought careers in the media, marketing and advertising:[5]

> I imagine I would move on as there are many opportunities and I certainly don't want to stay too long in one place . . . I want to do a bit of everything. I'll start off in radio and after that become news editor in radio, move on up into television and become a television reporter and after that become a news editor of television, and then become a director of current affairs in television. That will suit me when I'm a bit older and I want to do something with my life.

> Looking back at my past experiences, I've never stayed anywhere longer than a few years and, looking at the future, it doesn't look like anything is going to change, so at the moment I wouldn't really be looking for one stable kind of career-structured job, especially as they say from the beginning that the majority of people who come

out of Inner City in the area I'm studying – media and communications – can only expect to get part-time work anyway.

> Certainly in advertising you can get by like just over lunch time, but I think you can easily get other jobs because you have got a skill. You'd either have to be no good or unlucky not to get by, and if you are unlucky you can easily get a job elsewhere. You can easily move around. I mean people who move around a lot, you know, like in engineering or something, people respect good long stints in a company, whereas in graphic advertising you are almost expected to keep moving around. The idea is to keep moving and each time you move go for a pay rise. I think also you generally stand out on credibility in that you keep moving to better paid jobs, but often a better paid job is with bigger clients and bigger clients mean more boring accounts.

Moreover, unlike those students intent on making traditional bureaucratic careers within organizations, these students were constantly monitoring external market conditions for new opportunities. In such circumstances it paid to have a wide network of contacts and connections facilitated by attending the "right" schools, university, and belonging to the right kinds of club. This orientation was sometimes apparent in their attitudes towards higher education. One student at Home Counties University, for instance, was actively involved in an organization which encouraged links between students and business. He regarded the contacts and experience he had accumulated in such extracurricular activities as being of more practical importance than his subject of study, because they had "developed my CV a lot", in contrast to his studies in Management Studies which he thought had taught him "practically nothing". Although he recognized that getting a degree was crucial for "opening doors": "There are definite advantages to having a degree because employers' expectations are higher so they put you in the fast lane."

Likewise, "going through the private school network gives me certain advantages", upon which he did not elaborate. What our research evidence indicates is a close link between students who have flexible orientations and market power, derived through the acquisition of the appropriate stock of cultural capital such as family background, private schooling and attendance at one of the elite established universities, particularly Oxbridge. The "social" confidence involved in forfeiting the psychological security associated with a traditional bureaucratic career in favour of the "risks" involved in constructing a career portfolio is related to class, gender and academic biography. The small numbers involved in this study make it difficult to quantify, but the largest proportion of students with this "flexible" orientation was among males from middle-class backgrounds studying at Oxbridge. The vast majority of students with this orientation in the other two universities in this study were also from professional and managerial backgrounds. Indeed, in some instances they were sons whose fathers managed their own companies, which meant that if all else failed there was "always the possibility of expanding the family business". At Inner City only three students could be assigned to this category.

Whether these students continue to cherish the virtues of flexible and uncertain occupational careers when they have mortgaged homes and are in stable relationships is a moot point. However, what these students already acknowedge is that their partners are unlikely to have the same kinds of career, given a recognition that they will need a provider of household services and, more importantly, an emotional refuge from the strains of flexible work and career patterns. As a male student confessed, "It sounds like the Escort and 2.5 kids!".

The vast majority of the students we interviewed subscribed to orientations which we have labelled as either traditional bureaucratic or flexible. But there were a small number who can be distinguished as "entrepreneurial" in that they wanted to become self-employed or to set up their own businesses to exploit a niche in the market. Their limited number does not necessarily imply that the "enterprise culture" of the 1980s had been ignored by the students in our study. Some of those with flexible orientations envisaged starting their own businesses. The reason why it was not part of their immediate plans was because of a realistic understanding that they lacked the business experience, ideas, contacts and resources to start a successful venture. As these two students observed:

> I'd like to work for a small firm I think, but having said that, working in a large firm is very good for training, the first couple of years for experience and also for contacts as well. That's why maybe I wouldn't set up my own business straight away, go in, get some experience, contacts, then possible move on to my own thing.

I don't think it's so much that people don't *want* to start up small businesses, I think there's so much competition from multinationals and people that have cornered the market in particular commodities, that . . . for young companies to try and set up it is fiercely competitive. I don't think it's a lack of effort or that people don't want to do it, I think it's what you come up . . . against, and sort of, like the security you naturally have to have to start the business anyway, is going to have to come from a particular, you're going to have to come from a particular, social background to have that sort of money behind you, that sort of support. I mean, like, you could be a working-class man, with a very entrepreneurial idea or an enterprising scheme, but I mean you wouldn't be able to get it off the ground because you wouldn't have financial support, or you wouldn't have the contacts to be able to get a company like that set up, so it really leaves you with people that have got the collateral, they've got the security, the finance to be able to set up, or they know people that are going to be able to help them, so I think it's limited to particular groups of people that *can* be enterprising . . . We did have the enterprise scheme didn't we, though? Was it a thousand pounds . . . ?

Moreover, the handful of students who did exhibit an entrepreneurial orientation did not conform to the "loadsamoney" caricature. The only person who came close to this image was an Asian woman from Inner City:

I would like to fulfil myself. I mean everything you do, it's to fulfil yourself, to be someone and get somewhere, to do something with your life . . . So I would like to work for myself at the end of the day because then if you are successful or you fail, you only have to answer to yourself . . . If I have a business I don't want to be a partner with anybody. They can be my associates but not my partners. I know that's selfish but you have to be in this world. At the end of the day all I want to do is to be really big and have lots of money and I don't care where I do it . . . What's really important to me is a lot of money. That's what it boils down to at the end of the day. That is why I want to work for myself. Nobody became rich by working for other people.

As well as demonstrating a tradition of business ownership among sections of the Asian community (Aldrich et al. 1981), this response was explicable in terms of a reaction to family pressures to marry and to forgo her occupational ambition:

> I don't want to do what everybody else does. I don't want to just get a shop like my mum . . . My dad . . . thinks I'm mad. He's very old fashioned, very old fashioned. He says, "What's the point of having all these ideas?" Whenever I get something he always says it's risky. He's very unenterprising.

She has since left home and bought two houses which are being renovated with a view to selling. However, the financial pressures have forced her to take regular employment in a solicitor's office since graduation because at least, "you get paid at the end of the month. You can't do that buying and selling houses."

This emphasis on personal freedom and initiative was common to all the students in this category. They shared a belief that working for other people, especially in larger organizations, limited them as individuals:

> Well, there are ideas of the job that appeal to me, as it were, and there are ideas that don't, as in anything, and I'd like to put bits together but that can't happen. So if I was to give a run-down of the different things that were in my mind . . . I think in the Bar the advantages are that you are working for yourself, that's an element that I like; the atmosphere is extremely good; the work environment is friendly; and I enjoy the advocacy. That is one of the main reasons perhaps because I do love a verbal fight . . . I do enjoy the financial world very much, so that would be an area . . . I enjoy the teamwork element. I wouldn't in the end want to be working all my life for somebody else, because that's being negative, for example in an area like merchant banking, where it's very difficult to break out. You are, broadly speaking, as far as you can go to be head of a merchant bank and still you're not working for yourself, you're still a salaried employee, but that would be the negative side of that . . . The positives of management consultancy would be, and what I find fascinating, is the aspects of taking a company apart, I'd enjoy that very much. And I would enjoy the business side of things and if I wanted to go into that I would certainly think about taking another degree.

An entrepreneurial orientation was also expressed by a young black woman who believed that private enterprise was a way of overcoming the disadvantage experienced by minority groups. However, she believed that there was little likelihood of this becoming a reality, because:

> If you go to someone here with an idea, they don't encourage you; they find problems and instead of advising you on how you can overcome those problems, they use that as a reason not to risk their money financially. Whereas they should actually say yes more often and send in advisers to help to solve their problems. Not only would this encourage people, it would help them and so when they make money they'll help someone else. They need to encourage the people with the money to support more people without the money who want to set up their own businesses and work out a way to get their money back but that doesn't happen.

The problem of getting started in business had been overcome by a student from Home Counties who had been running (with a partner) a small business employing 10 men in the offshore oil industry throughout his three years of university study. However:

> I find it terrible the fact that one might say I was in fact becoming a part of the "enterprise culture"; because I believe Mrs Thatcher had completely the wrong idea of what a business is. It's not a matter of personal aggrandizement and self-valorization. Like, just because I happen to be the employer of these people, it just makes me another worker really because, especially in the oil industry, it's a massively tiered and hierarchical structure where everyone works for someone else and is both an employer and an employee. The people who work for us, for instance, are all self-employed. We're all cogs in a big machine.

Another Inner City student had also become self-employed while studying, through "pyramid selling". In this case, it was not seen simply as an entrepreneurial venture, but as a way of life which was leading him to abandon his studies. As he explained it,

> We're all self-employed. We just help everyone to become self-employed . . . I am in a leadership rôle. I have my own network but there are no bosses in this business. No one can tell anyone what to

do . . . Good management is to be part of a team, I believe, and to have everybody working together for a common goal, letting people develop their own initiative for the common goal . . . Management by consensus . . . Leadership skills, leading by example . . . to be doing something rather than sitting around in your office and to be able to help people achieve what they want to achieve, not what I want them to achieve . . . It's not like traditional capitalism where you think, "Who can I rip off next?" it's "who can I help next?". In this business it's all about personal growth because people have to learn how to communicate, how to develop confidence, self-discipline and to really employ themselves, and to really achieve any of that it's all about personal growth and self-awareness. I don't regard it as work. It's my life.

What the entrepreneurial category reveals is the range and complexity of motivations, drives and aspirations which these students demonstrate. Nevertheless, in general terms we have argued that they show little resistance or counter-cultural tendencies towards challenging the dominance of work, careers, and material wealth. Indeed, they share a sense that they can find satisfaction, challenge and enjoyment within existing institutional arrangements. However, this was not true for all the students in this study. There was a very small number of students who were not willing to conform to the hegemony of the career.

Turning to these few "non-conformists" which we found in our study, there are the "drop-outs" who characteristically are "unconventional" in lifestyle and opinions, and who may contribute to a class of "lumpen intellectuals". Such students can be found in all three of the universities of our study. As one mature female Home Counties student related:

I've done loads of different jobs – shop, bar, run my own business, model in art college for years, market stalls, own shop, gardening business with friends – I still do that one day a week. Peripheral sorts of jobs – I've never done a proper job.

Nor did she intend to have a "proper" job now she had her degree. For another of this very small category:

The thought of a career makes me cringe. I wouldn't like to be restricted into doing one thing for the rest of my life. If I was to go into the public sector – social work or something like that – I'd find the system quite hard to handle.

Instead, she intended to join a local Christian commune working as a volunteer. Another student emphasized the boredom and futility of working for other people:

> I find work boring, work for other people boring . . . if you're going to worry about work, other people's work, you know, it's just not on. The object of life is happiness . . . for me it means really . . . , mucking about with electronics, technical whatever, um, going out, seeing things . . . In London, this is what I miss about London really is the museums, you know, you can spend hours in them, . . . yeah, that's, that's life, it's like absorption, um, working for other people is completely a waste of time – waste of one's *own* time . . . Because it's non-productive. It's, it's producing things for other people, you know, other people reaping the benefits . . . Being told *what* to do, *how* to do it, *when* to do it . . . it's not on.

Although such attitudes were evident in our study, there was little evidence of the counter-cultural perspectives more commonly found among the student population in the 1960s (Keniston 1965). Equally, in our interviews it was difficult to find any students who subscribed to *ritualist* perspectives, with the possible exception of two female students:

> Well, I think what I really want to do is to be useful and help people, which is probably my medical background. Pay isn't important, I wouldn't think about the public sector if it was. I suppose security is quite important, that's why I've chosen to be a solicitor rather than barrister, because at least as a solicitor if you're ill or want time off for maternity or whatever, you still get paid, whereas as a barrister if you don't work, you don't get paid. I really think that's about it. I don't really have any feelings about self-fulfilment or anything like that. I don't think I'd get that from law or a job; I'd get that from friends.

The second was a French student who had quit *grand école* and had come to Home Counties to study English and French literature "to have more freedom to study what I wanted". She wanted to become a self-employed writer:

It's not a question of attraction but of vocation, something I've always wanted to do. Practically, I think I'm going to have to go into secretarial work for a time. Also, there's a possibility of doing an MA next term and typing people's manuscripts; you could get by in that.

She was clearly not committed to a career or to the idea of making money, although she realized that other options offered little financial security:

The rest of society seems geared towards job security; everyone else is looking for that, or so you see and read and hear on the telly but I've never wanted a nine-to-five job. I think if you want to be self-employed in anything you balance on the edge much more because a secure job provides the peace of mind to do other things but there's a lot more excitement in doing your own thing and being paid for it. You have to have a healthy self-respect just to think that you have something to say that other people will want to read. I would balance home and work. It's horrible thinking of giving priority to either. They're also mutually dependent. I think it's the case in any job; if you're happier at home you'll work better and if you're happy in your job your home is better. It'll be harder to balance the two if you work at home because you have to define a space and time to work in. That's what's so much fun about it, you have to have the discipline to do it. The hardest thing about writing or being self-employed in general is getting yourself to do it. Self-motivation is a much greater part of self-employment than if it's all organized for you through your work.

We have argued that many of those with a traditional bureaucratic orientation upheld the professional ideal of service to the community. What separates the "socially committed" from them is a total disregard for their own personal careers and material rewards. Indeed, their aims often involved attempting to subvert organizational goals in the interests of such things as the women's movement, ecology movement, trade unionism, socialism, or religious sects. Only a handful of students held this orientation and among our interviewees they comprised four women and one man, all from Inner City University. These students did not intend to "drop-out" but sought employment, or voluntary work, as a means for pursuing the causes they espoused:

Voluntary work with the Church of the Brethren working with refugees in the USA. It isn't finalized yet. I'm doing things that will be helping people in some way 'cos the Church of the Brethren, it isn't a religious organization as such. It's working for peace and a better world.

Also, a mature student who had been studying the economic under-development of the Third World was very clear about her own position in an imperialist society as a black, working-class woman. She therefore had an alternative conception of a "career" and of "success", which contrasted with the usual view of management as:

the ability to identify with the company more than with the workers and their ability to control their staff. That's good from the point of view of the company. It's impossible for them to be good from the point of view of the workers, or they won't stay managers very long!

Similarly, another mature student, who had studied psychotherapy, explained:

in the world of industrial management you are looking for someone who will deny a lot of the human qualities of the workforce . . . The motivation is not humanistic but material, to look after their investment in that individual, to keep someone functioning in a situation in which individuals become estranged and alienated, all for the artificial coinage of a thing called money. I believe at one point Freud called money the excrement of society. There's no humanistic exchange taking place there. It's got no real value.

Each of these people had entered higher education after some years in routine employment. One of them now worked in a local council-funded women's centre that she had become involved with while studying.

I'm receptionist, bookings clerk, responsible for the security of the building, plus I'm responsible for the image of the building, making sure that the information we put out – our leaflets – are up to date and I've got to do something about the image of the building – redecorate it . . . I think I'll probably stay there, get experience and then move on somewhere else, but I'd still like to keep in touch with what's going on there, like, keep involved.

She does aspire to a management position but her reasons have little

111

to do with social status or money. It is seen as a way of gaining the "clout" to challenge relations at work:

> I think it is different women managing from men managing, because I think a lot of women, whether they like to admit it or not, if one of the male councillors or officials came in and asked for something, they'd do it quicker because he's a man. It's all down to condition- ing because everyone assumes that a manager is a man for a start and I think a woman has to work harder at gaining respect. She has to prove a lot more that she's capable of doing things before peo- ple will believe that she's capable of getting on with things. I think some things would be different if women were running everything.

From this discussion, it is clear that there are a variety of orien- tations towards the labour market among university students. Accord- ing to the interviews we conducted at Oxbridge, Home Counties and Inner City, there is an overwhelming tendency for them to adopt *conformist* perspectives. In this, there has probably been a change in overall student attitudes since the 1960s. Obviously, a number of factors account for this, ranging from ongoing economic recession and the tighter labour market conditions in which students expect to find themselves, the need to find employment in order to reduce bank overdrafts and to repay loans that were used to finance their higher education, to changes in the nature of student culture and subcul- tures. The ideological impact of Marxism, for example, with its offer of alternative non-capitalist realities, which was pronounced among some student groups in the 1960s and 1970s, is now almost dead. The demise of the Soviet Union has reaffirmed to students that their futures are within an established socio-economic and political order which is unlikely to move in the direction of the more utopian or radi- cal appeals that they may still encounter at university.

However, within the prodominent conformist perspective it is per- haps surprising that our respondents overwhelmingly subscribed to what we have described as a traditional bureaucratic orientation to the labour market. Despite large-scale organizational restructuring, the greater insecurities of managerial and professional employment, and the widespread rhetoric of the enterprise culture, most students continued to search for long-term careers within the shelter of large corporations that are still seen to offer them predictable increments in status, responsibilities and rewards. Accordingly, it is our opinion that the majority of university graduates are ill-prepared for the realities of work in the 1990s, despite closer links between the universities and employer organizations, and the introduction of the Enterprise in Higher Education Initiative. Such government-inspired innovations appear to have had limited impact upon the attitudes and values of students. Indeed, it seems that among those we interviewed, it was those students from more privileged backgrounds who were the most likely to have "flexible" orientations to the labour market. Most of these students were white males studying at Oxbridge, or in some instances at Home Counties, and on the basis of our interviews the development of a "flexible" orientation was closely linked to student preceptions of their relative position in the market for superior jobs. Accordingly, it is these students who appear to be most in tune with the changing market conditions for graduate labour and to possess the requisite cultural capital which underlies the reproduction of class divisions in corporate recruitment processes, despite the increasing number of women and those from ethnic and working-class origins who now attend IHEs. But how do corporate recruiters perceive their selection processes and the criteria which they adopt for hiring those who are likely to become corporate leaders in the future? It is to this question that we turn our attention in the next chapter.

Notes

1. This is clearly not true for a growing number of university staff employed on short-term contracts. A statistical report compiled by the Association of University Teachers (1990) states:

   Over 60,000 academic and related staff now work in UK universities. Of these less than half are lecturers or professors. Although there has been an overall 40 per cent increase in total staff since 1970/1, and a 10 per cent increase since 1979/80, this has been almost entirely in non-university-funded research staff. Total numbers of non-wholly-university-funded staff have more than trebled, rising from 5300 in 1970 to 19,336 today. One in three university staff are now not paid from university funds: the great majority of them are research staff on short-term contracts.

2. Some of the students we interviewed remained vague about the specific occupations they hoped to enter, although their general orientations, discussed in this chapter, were more explicit. In part, this is explained by Bourdieu and Passeron (1964) as a result of an academic education in

113

which students and staff collude "to conceal from themselves a future which might well take away all meaning from their present" (p. 59). This may certainly be true in the knowledge that in the present market for graduate labour many of the students in this study will not be able to get into the kinds of career they were hoping for, and in many cases expecting to achieve. Moreover, the intrusion of the reality of finding employment comes as a shock to some of these students. A female Home Counties student of English literature, for example, recalled that the only mention of a future career came "In my second year, when a lecturer on Dickens said, 'Well, of course, those of you who are going to join the Civil Service . . . ' and I thought, 'Oh my God, is that the sort of thing we're expected to do?'." One reaction to this situation was to put off decisions until the last minute, after examinations usually, so as to "worry about one thing at a time".

3. Moreover, access to privileged knowledge is an aspect of professionalism likely to have been stressed by higher education lecturers defining their teaching in compliance with the requirements of professional bodies and, increasingly, defining their own work according to specified measures of "quality", although this is in fact also characteristic of non-professional craft working. A true profession can only be defined in terms of its ability to regulate entry to the profession and to maintain standards within it, as is the case of the British Medical Association for doctors and the Bar Council for lawyers. Teaching and social work, though they do not correspond to this more rigorous and exact definition of professionalism, were among student interviewees the archetypes of professional occupations.

4. This contributes to what Larson (1977) also called "the professional mystique", which is "complemented by secrecy" and enhanced by the claim to "expert knowledge" that higher education has historically been instrumental in communicating and validating. Larson notes that the claim to professional status on the basis of "expert" knowledge is ambiguous, therefore a more readily identifiable characteristic of professionals is that they are members of socially dominant groups (p. xvi). In particular, professionals are outside and above traditional manual working-class people they by and large serve, and who accept that professionals possess superior ability and knowledge that is in general validated by higher education. It is therefore no coincidence that the current demystification of professionalism, which holds teachers, doctors and other professional public servants increasingly accountable through more explicit contracts with the consumers of their previously self-regulated services, has occurred at the same time that more people have been able to gain access to "expert" knowledge through the expansion of higher education and the dismantling of the traditional welfare bureaucracies (including education)

114

that have sustained the growth of the professional or "service class" since the Second World War (Perkin 1989).

5. Bourdieu and Passeron (1964, pp. 87–8) have noted the attraction of the media, marketing and advertising for "those sons and daughters of the bourgeoisie who are threatened with down-classing as these are the newly emerging professions in the newest sectors of cultural and artistic production, such as the big public and private organizations engaged in cultural production (radio, TV, marketing, advertising, social science research, and so on), where jobs and careers have not yet acquired the rigidity of the older bureaucratic professions and recruitment is generally done by co-option, i.e. on the basis of "connections" and affinities of habits, rather than formal qualifications . . . positions halfway between studenthood and a profession . . . for which specific qualifications (e.g. a diploma in film making, or a sociology or psychology degree) are a genuine ticket of entry only for those who are able to supplement the official qualifications with the real – social – qualifications". What Bourdieu and Passeron clearly failed to anticipate is the shift away from bureaucratic models of organization, and the appeal of careers in these industries even for those who are not in danger of "down-classing". It was doubtful whether many Home Counties or Inner City graduates would be able to supplement their official qualifications with the unofficial connections and common cultural abilities that made up what has been seen at Oxbridge as the real, untaught, and transferable skills of class inheritance, to secure entry into the media. The one Inner City media hopeful was clearer about what she was going to do and how she was going to do it, partly because she was older and had worked her way through college as the self-employed manager of a company hiring roadies to heavy metal bands while contributing to the student and music press and so had assembled a portfolio as well as experience in video production.

"Getting in" was recognized by all aspirants for "the media" as a major problem. Competition, even for one-year, postgraduate journalism courses, let alone in-house training schemes, was intense, and in any case did not guarantee employment, any more than the many specialized degree courses in journalism, typically burgeoning in higher education just as the actual opportunities for employment are rapidly collapsing (see Ainley, B. 1993). The only alternative was to begin as a self-employed freelance worker and hope to "get in" from there.

CHAPTER SIX

The adaptive paradigm and employer recruitment strategies

Recruitment into managerial, professional and other highly paid jobs is a decisive determinant of a persons material life chances. Thus the question of who gets appointed to such positions is central to our understanding of the social reproduction of the class structure. This issue is particularly important, because we are interested in understanding the impact of the shift from bureaucratic to adaptive organizational paradigms on the articulation between higher education and the labour market. To what extent have changes in organizational models affected recruiters' criteria of the necessary competences required for professional, managerial and executive positions? Within this context, how important are educational credentials in the recruiting process and how far has the shift to adaptive models of organization enlarged the range of opportunities available to university graduates?

The recruiters we spoke to were disarmingly detailed about the mechanics of their recruitment processes, and equally disarmingly vague about who actually gets recruited. This was especially true with any mention of class, gender, and racial differences in their pattern of selection. It was therefore difficult to delve beneath the professional rhetoric that currently gravitates around notions of personal and transferable skills. With this caveat in mind, what could be gleaned from these interviews offers highly suggestive evidence of the changing significance of cultural capital in corporate organizations.

Many of the 30 recruiters we interviewed in 16 large and medium sized organizations were aware of recent changes in the way they were thinking about their human resource needs. The reasons stated for such changes varied from a complete restructuring of the organization and its markets, to little more than an increased emphasis on team-work and project management. International competition, techno-logical innovation, changing product markets and, in the public sector, the creation of quasi-markets and competitive tendering, were all cited as reasons for rethinking their human resource strategies:

> We were very much a hierarchically-driven company with large blocks of hierarchies, sometimes in conflict with each other. The development side, the manufacturing side, the sales support side of the company, the many little pyramids within these big pyramids. A classic organization . . . Ten years ago we prided ourselves on being a maker of clever boxes. Technology was the king and, I'm exaggerating, but to sell things to customers was important but that was a thing you thought after you'd invented this wonderful piece of technology. We had a horrible shock in the early eighties and nearly went bankrupt. The consequence of that is the strategy which we put in place in the early eighties, we've continued to develop since then and will continue to do so now. Which means being customer oriented, having an absolute dedication to quality, and although people are still proud of their own personal professional-ism, if you like, as a technologist or something else, it's in a frame-work which enables you to work maybe competitively but not in a destructive way. I'm being simplistic about this because at any one time there will be conflicts and differences of view, and so on, so I think it has bound the company together. Certainly in the early eighties, just to give one example, we put a lot of effort into train-ing people in how to handle change, the process of change. Although we still do that it's not nearly as important as it used to be because we're so used to it now. It happens all the time. At least once a month there will be a major reorganization of some kind. You keep little lists of who's doing what and they're always being changed. It's accepted as part of the way of life. (Information Technology)

> Particularly over the last decade or so we've been moving away from that, low technology and low value added goods, into higher added value, higher technology goods . . . At one time we used to recruit metallurgists. Now we don't need metallurgists. We need produc-tion engineers and electrical engineers to help us make what we make cheaper and better than the competition . . . We want good engineers who are going to run and manage the business in the

future . . . Again the sales and marketing people that we recruit are different sorts of people. Selling metals you could afford to have a fairly low technology animal out there. He didn't need to be all that bright. Now, they need a good technological background because they're talking to architects and designers and you can't send out some guy who flogs pencils . . . All our marketing sales people are engineers first. (Industrial Holding Company)

Local government services now are having to become more commercially managed, and you may well find that people with financial management skills and with people management skills will be sought after for running commercially oriented services, like a leisure services department or refuse collection, where they have to go out and tender with contracts and keep trading accounts, and that's going to come into legal services, it's going to come into personnel perhaps, a whole range of services. Now that could open up they way for people from the private sector, people with other appropriate qualifications to come into very senior positions within those departments, and very particularly, I think, with financial management skills. (Metropolitan Council)

In much of the research literature, the analysis of employer recruitment procedures begins by making a distinction between: "functionally specific criteria of suitability, which relate to competence or ability to do the job in question, and functionally non-specific criteria of acceptability which relate to wider organizational matters such as 'stability', 'reliability', and 'predictability', in short, the degree to which the worker is habituated to employment or otherwise organizationally acceptable" (Jenkins 1985, 170).[1] On the basis of our interviews the distinction between suitability and acceptability does facilitate an understanding of employer recruitment practices. However, the shift from bureaucratic to adaptive paradigms of organization effectively undermines the equation "suitability equals job specific skills", because job tasks are subject to rapid change, and efficient job performance is seen to depend upon generic transferable personal skills as much as specific job-related skills. Moreover, given that the recruitment criteria of employers were explicitly targeting people who had the potential to rise to managerial positions, the individuals "capability" to develop was an equally important feature of employer deliberations. Therefore, on the basis of our empirical evidence, it is

118

necessary to distinguish three interrelated aspects of their selection process – *suitability*, *capability* and *acceptability*.

Suitability

Suitability involves the basic competence to "get the job done". However, given that the job to be done is likely to change radically and rapidly because of technological innovation, changes in product markets, and organizational redesign, the criteria of suitability now incorporates communication and personal skills along with the necessary technical competences. Therefore, the criteria of suitability will vary significantly, depending upon the nature of the company in question and the specific job to be filled (Roizen and Jepson 1985). For some occupations, such as accountancy, marketing, and industrial relations, the emphasis is almost exclusively on personal and transferable skills. In the scientific, engineering and research areas, although there is a greater emphasis on technical competence to do the job, there is no less a recognition that personal and "people" skills are a vital ingredient of performance.

There was a consensus among those we spoke to that it was no longer a question of recruiting people who would perform routine even if highly skilled tasks, in stable conditions. It was no longer a case of appointing some new cogs for an old bureaucratic machine, where tasks were predetermined, clearly defined, and individually performed. People had to be flexible, adaptable and willing to engage in regular retraining and professional development programmes. One of our respondents suggested that in some respects the emphasis on non-technical skills was simply "flavour of the month":

> The whole question of developing a model of competences is something which is fairly recent in organizations. I suppose like a lot of things, it's flavour of the month but it does make you sit down and think what are the latent skills which a senior manager has got. What makes a senior manager? (Retail Bank)

But if the attempt to compose a model of competences is flavour of the month, the basic ingredients are not so ephemeral. The reason why the definition of "suitability" has come to incorporate non-specific work attributes and abilities is due to the shift to adaptive and flexible organizational structures:

If people have a love of learning, who are prepared to accept the fact that the skills that they have today are going to be redundant tomorrow and they need to reskill, if they've got that sort of attitude, then you're okay. It's this need for adaptability and flexibility, the need to be prepared to relearn and to learn new skills that is more important in some senses than the skills they've actually got today. Most computer science students, for example, when they come out of their degree course are 'way, 'way behind where we are technically – because the state of the art is moving on so fast and we're in that field. (Information Technology)

When I first took over graduate recruitment we were looking at people developing into specific managerial rôles. Now I think that's going to be less the case. The training is moving into a far more generalist base where they will see a lot of different functions. There will still be the ones who want to go on the more specialized route but I think there will be more and more the case where they're going to go across company boundaries and see different techniques and apply the same managerial skills but in different situations. (Retail Bank)

It was also acknowledged that there was a demand for good generic skills, including verbal and written communications, numeracy and a hands-on knowledge of personal computers, irrespective of the job in question.[2]

I suppose you're looking for how well they've handled things like, how good is their numeracy? . . . We try to assess their ability to write. In a way, we're not looking for people who are necessarily creative writers, but we're looking for people who can actually put words together well and will not make errors, because if you think in terms of preparation of brochure input, you don't want it littered with mistakes and grammatical errors. (Leisure Group)

Bottom up we look for very good communication skills . . . Numeracy, fluency, and some basic personal skills like being able to write reports, give presentations, and so on. (Information Technology)

Obviously they'd have to have (depending on which part of the operation they're in) a basic technical qualification and a minimum of a 2:1, that sort of level of excellence . . . You actually find yourself relating to people in NewYork (head office), relating to the managing director here as well as your peers, so you have to be able to present your case concisely so written and verbal communication is most important. (Pharmaceutical)

Obviously IT skills are important and there are very few offices in our local government that don't have PCs on desks, very few systems that aren't computerized. So that's clearly an area. (Metropolitan Council)

I think we need people who are able to use computing and are not afraid of using PCs and doing analysis on PCs, but not having to be programmers in any way. We don't train our marketing people to write programmes, but they may be using things like Lotus and doing spreadsheet work which I think is important. (Leisure Group)

Despite the fact that having the necessary competences increasingly depends upon good personal skills, the importance of an established expert knowledge base should not be underestimated, especially in industries which depend on the application of advanced technical and scientific knowledge, for instance in the pharmaceutical industry or in the field of information technology. In some cases there was clear evidence that the level of technical competence was on the increase because of the introduction of advanced technologies and more complex work processes (Block 1990). In accountancy, for instance:

If we consciously said, "What we want is people who will be good at going out ticking and bashing and checking out computer printouts and then we'll throw them (the students) away after that", then I think we'd be misperceiving the nature of accountancy, the professionalism now because we don't actually need the first-year students to anything like the same extent as we did do because auditing is changing, computers are helping to release drudgery; there's more planning and thinking about how to look at the clients business and not simply blanketing with every student in sight and pulling out every file in sight and ticking and bashing it. So the trick now is going to be to get our students through the first year or two, giving them experience which may not be charged out to clients fully but to enable them to gain the knowledge and experience to become more responsible later on. (Accountancy Partnership)

Similarly in the motor industry:

> Technology really has come in – robotics, computer-controlled equipment, etc. This requires a much higher level of sophistication in terms of the engineers who are servicing it. This is on the manufacturing side. On the other side, you have the research and development people and here they're looking at the next generation of cars. It's all become very complex. It's become more and more like the aircraft industry in a sense. So we're having to look and say "Do we require the 2:2 with bags of interpersonal skills? Do we now need to look seriously for 2:1s and first class honours people?", because that's what the technology is starting to demand. (Industrial Manufacturer)

Here, it would seem that the criteria of suitability is defined in terms of the technical competence of the new recruit because of the increasing complexity of work practices, but even so our respondent went on to say:

> But at the end of the day, the company is about managing situations, even if they're technical situations, so you'll never, in my view, go for the pure university boffin who just wants to lock himself into a corner and not be bothered by other people – if there is such a person . . . There is no doubt that our emphasis is shifting towards higher academic qualifications, but still the most important things are the usual managerial skills. We're looking for people who have leadership qualities, good interpersonal skills. (Industrial Manufacturer)

A recruiter in the field of information technology also told us:

> I think the days of the long, tall, thin "teccy" who can't talk to anybody else have gone, if ever they were there anyway. I think we need broad-based business people on the one hand who are IT competent, but we do need technologists who have broad good personal skills as well. So it's a bit of both . . . so, you need both a technologist who can talk to people, and a business person who's competent about technology.

What these quotations highlight is the way in which the criteria of "suitability" is not only demanding an increase in the technical competence to do the job, but also the fact that adequate job performance also depends upon the development of flexible personal skills. One of the main reasons for this is that, irrespective of the task to be performed, they will be expected to work efficiently in project teams:

> Team work is one of the shocks when one ceases full-time education which is all based on the individual performing as an individual and competing with other people at all times and then to walk into an arena where you cannot get anything done unless you work as part of a team. You can't do your work in isolation. You have to work in teams . . . Teamwork is, I think, an essential skill in any modern industry. (Petro-chemicals)

> Drucker actually saw it in the seventies when he was talking about the specialisms of people coming together in task forces, that's exactly what happens, particularly in our industry. You have people who are brought together for short periods of time, break up and go into other groups. The need to understand teams and how they operate; your preferred rôle, what it is that you have to offer and to bring. All those things are vital for people who are going to have to live in that environment. (High Technology Company)

> In the accounting area, a manager is a manager of people, leading teams and getting the best out of those teams. And those teams are changing from job to job. It's not the same set of people. They've got to be able to co-ordinate the work of the team against budget, for example. They've got to be able to liaise with the client. And that means co-ordinating the teams efforts to get the job done with the client to a deadline. What they haven't got to be is overly aggressive, overly abrasive people for whom leadership means "I'm the only person who matters; over the hill with me, boys" [sic], because the client is not the enemy. The client is the person we're trying to work with and the competition, if we're trying to beat the competition, which obviously we're trying to do, you don't do it by individual managers going round doing their own thing. (Accountancy Partnership)

> In an administrative rôle . . . in local government . . . you're working in teams. You have to work with other people. You have to be able to work for other people. And you'll have other people working for you, later if not sooner. And you also have to work with the public: telephone, reception, dealing with complaints, people from all kinds

of backgrounds, dissatisfied customers. (Metropolitan Council)

In the world of work you're very rarely working alone. You're almost always a part of a team. There are other parts of the operation which depend on you doing your work. And that applies to every individual. (Accountancy Partnership)

In the shift from bureaucratic to adaptive models of organization, the criteria of suitability leads to a greater emphasis on being able to work in and manage project teams (Kanter 1989; Handy 1989). In the adaptive paradigm of organization the question of "leadership" takes on added importance given that the nature of this is seen to depend less upon bureaucratic authority than on charisma, personal example and face-to-face consultation:

The definition of leadership would be the ability for the individual we're interviewing to be able to guide or direct a group of people or an individual, whether it be a peer, superior, or subordinate towards a task or goal without necessarily relying on authority . . . It's very easy to show leadership skills if, say, you're a teacher because the students are going to listen to you whatever you say. If you say, "Jump upside down on your chair" and they'll do it. Now that is not leadership skill; that's relying on your authority. If you're working in a group of peers, or better still, if you're working with a boss, whether it be work experience or maybe your tutor, and you're able to get them to do something for you quite cleverly, then we believe that's a good example of leadership. The reason I mentioned that is because you said about team work earlier on, it's no good if you just ask someone to do something because you're the manager. You won't get the most out of people. You won't be able to get the team behind you. And what we want is people who will abide by and follow your decision irrespective of your position. And that's what's important for us in a team, to get the respect of the staff and therefore be able to perform sometimes the more difficult tasks, and make the more difficult decisions which you wouldn't be able to do if you hadn't got the respect. So we're deliberately there looking for an angle on people which may not be the same as other peoples definition of leadership. So it's all related back to the job. (Retail Store)

The Japanese . . . they've been so successful because of consultation as opposed to telling. They have a very different culture to ours. It's a consultative culture. Everyone works in groups. Now we can't afford to ignore that. We're moving towards that. We're trying hard. The company is trying to adopt a more consultative approach. In plants now, whenever there is an appointment of a senior manager, interpersonal skills, consultative ability is far higher up the agenda than it used to be. The managers that are going into plants now are very much more sophisticated people than they were 10 to 15 years ago when they tended to be big, bull elephants who were frightening, and ruled by fear. (I'm generalizing though as there have always been exceptions.) So there's been a very powerful culture change even within this company. (Industrial Manufacturer)

Five or six years ago, we were only looking at about five different qualities. They were breadth of vision, imagination, analysis, sense of realities. And at that time we had leadership ability. But the definition of leadership ability encompassed a number of the other things which are now separated out as being separate kinds of qualities that we're looking at. So, leadership is also partly about the drive that a person has to get things done and the motivation that they can put on to other people, and how they delegate. That is part of leadership. (Petro-chemicals)

Capability

In adaptive models of organization the selection of students for fast-track training programmes leads recruiters to attach considerable importance to criteria of capability. This not only includes an assessment of the candidate's existing personal development or academic achievement but also, crucially, their potential for senior corporate positions. This is because they are looking to recruit future "leaders", although their potential is always assessed in terms of the students ability to quickly "add value" to the employing organization.

"Potential partner" is what we should be looking for and our interviewers are trained to think in those terms: can you see this person having the abilities – however one defines them at the moment – to go much further than simply the level of qualifying, because that is where the future of the business lies, in developing people who will be promotable to those top levels. (Accountancy Partnership)

We would be looking for people initially specifically for technical jobs . . . So they would come in and go and join retail banking or they would go into personnel function or they would go into finance. But in addition to having the necessary skills that we think we can develop to fulfil those positions then we would also look for the senior management characteristics as well as part of that. (Retail Bank)

The object . . . is to take a small number of good-calibre people and give them appropriate training and development with the aim of placing them [in jobs], and that they will arrive eventually at least at middle manager level within the organization and hopefully higher than that. That's the overall aim. (Industrial Holding Company)

We'd look for somebody who has the ability to come in and do a scientific job and to grow on that, so has potential to develop further on the skills and the knowledge that they've gained in that time of tertiary education. (Pharmaceuticals)

We pay up-front about £35–£40,000 per person for each of the 900-1000 we take in each year. But they are fee-earning from the start. But I would remind you that they are clever, highly educated people and they learn quickly, and they're motivated to learn quickly. So they become very valuable and by the time they're qualified they're fully operational. (Accountancy Partnership)

Most of those we interviewed felt that in order to satisfy their criteria of capability they were engaged in a selection process dedicated to identifying "the best of the bunch". The perceived need to recruit "the best" was motivated by changes in the working environment; technological innovation, for instance, was leading to a demand for more "intelligent" and flexible people because they are seen to be more likely to deal successfully in an innovative setting because of their ability to see the bigger picture, and to subject problems to detailed analysis rather than having to rely on "the way we've always done things" (see Gordon 1983, Zuboff 1989).

You can't turn a biologist into a chemist. There are things that you can do but basically if the people have only got one leg to stand on and you take that leg away, then you're going to have to rebuild another leg from scratch. So what we would ideally like to have, if we had an ideal world, is to develop the people, or get the people in the first place who've got more than one leg so if you chop one leg off they've still got the other one to stand on while you develop them in a different direction. (Petro-chemicals)

The foreman is not going to come up with any earth-shaking ideas. He's not going to improve the operation dramatically. But . . . he is going to generally keep things jogging along nicely. And his experience over the years is going to mean that if we get a particular problem . . . he will know from experience, "We've had this before. This was what it was" . . . Coupled with that, if he was wrong, he would probably still think that that was the answer and keep plugging away at something, rather than going back and thinking and analysing it properly. And that has probably nothing to do with graduates and foremen, just level of intelligence and the way they approach problems. (Pharmaceuticals)

The criteria of capability consisted of two key elements. The first was an assessment of "raw talent", "intellect", and "quality of mind", because "They've got to have a good brain, basically". Although it was generally acknowledged that graduate training schemes could do a lot to develop and polish the technical and personal skills which were required, there was a strong sense that this could not compensate for "raw talent". There was evidence of an underlying Darwinian view of the world, in which the job of the recruiter was to identify, on rational and objective grounds, those people who were a breed apart, given an innate quality of mind:

You can't change a million years of evolution in a week's course so you're looking for promising potential . . . Of course, we have training programmes which are designed to develop the skills and polish them up and that goes on for the rest of their managerial lives. (Industrial Manufacturer)

We look for intelligence. I'm not a psychologist but I am coming to the view that intellectually capable people are probably more able to cope with some of the traumas we throw at them, all other things being equal, than might otherwise be the case, because they can acquire new skills, perhaps they can see through the problems that are being thrown at them. (Information Technology)

It's almost that mix between super-intelligent and crackers! (Leisure Group)

Secondly, in the assessment of capability:

The whole ethos of universities and polytechnics is to say that "because you are doing a degree, therefore you have the capability". And academic capability is, I think, not enough. (Accountancy Partnership)

The reason being that it is not only a question of whether they've got the "innate" intellectual ability, but whether they have that "added something"; the internal drive, energy, and ambition to "make things happen", to be a "shaper" rather than a "follower". There is a perceived need to recruit people who have shaped their own worlds in ways that were out of the ordinary. The assumption being that if they have shown evidence of those additional qualities, they will be more likely to contribute to innovative environments rather than conform to traditional practices. In this respect, a vital aspect of capability is evidence of a charismatic personality. In Chapter 2 we defined this as consisting of a set of personal characteristics which are not reserved for a very small group of political, religious, or intellectual leaders, but more generally apply to those who seek to break the mould of routine actions and rule-following behaviour. They are the creators of new orders and are able to lead or work collectively through consultation and negotiation rather than through the imposition of bureaucratic authority:

You want someone who is going to change the world, or change things from what they are and be able to be critical of what we've got, but to be able to do it constructively, so that they're not an irritant. You want someone in a way who is almost like the sand in the oyster, that produces the pearl. But you want them to have the grit to sort of get the information from somebody and to say, "Look, I think you ought to do it this way", but not to upset them in doing it. A lot of the time you're working in teams and I think you want to achieve the end result but if you say, "Look, I don't think this is right. I think this is the way it should be going", you want them to influence it, but you don't want them to upset their colleagues while they're about it. (Leisure Group)

It's someone who's coming with a degree of vision. It's the leadership issue . . . they've already begun to say "this is the job I've been given to do but I could do it better by doing it differently". They understand the instructions that have been given but could make more of it and will suggest things that will add value . . . The people of the future are those who are driving the new technical way in which an audit is done. The way in which it's done you'd think was the same and would always stay the same but in the ten years since I qualified, life's changed enormously and the people who are now leading are those who had the vision five or six years ago to say "we don't have to do it this way. We can still achieve the same objective in another way". (Accountancy Partnership)

We're not particularly academically fussy. We want graduates for a number of reasons and many of those are personal reasons: they're self-motivated, independent, got to plan and organize their own time, got to be motivated to achieve their goals without being pushed. (Retail Store)

You can spot people who've been active in sports clubs or have taken part in lots of union linked activities where they've been treasurer or secretaries and where they've had to get on with everybody, organize things, they've had to produce books to account for their funding. When you meet people like that they have this little bit extra. (Accountancy Partnership)

We're not looking for succession planning to see who's going to be the next research director, for instance, at that sort of level. But we are looking as part of a personal spec. for people who've made contributions outside of just being a participant or a taker. So people who've given something like, whether it be they've organized trips on Inter-rail or whether they've been a treasurer or something of some society. So they're people who show some potential. (Pharmaceuticals)

We're looking for people who are task oriented, who show evidence of having done something with their lives. You can have a graduate who gets a 2:1 but if you look deeper and you're looking for evidence of creativity, initiative, drive, and there is a blank on the rest of his application, then that gives you certain concerns. But if you see someone who's organized himself on a world tour, who's organized the local scout group, who's been doing things; it doesn't matter what it is – it can be doing things in a church, being a church warden at the age of 18; what is important is that they've actually got away from the television and done something. You're looking for evidence of have they been on committees, have they been prefects, what have they done outside, have they organized golf competitions, have they done charity things? (Industrial Manufacturer)

Acceptability

What our discussion so far reveals is a significant shift in employer criteria of recruitment. This is because in adaptive paradigms of organization what is necessary to get jobs done increasingly depends upon personal skills and compatibility. The criteria of acceptability concerns the degree of "social fit" in terms of outlook, interests, connections, style, dress, speech, which provide the "personal chemistry" required for a smooth transition into the organizations way of doing things, based on personal compatibility with colleagues and clients

If they seem to be broadly suitable, there are three things I'd be looking for: technical competence – what evidence is there that they are professionally competent? Do I think they would have managerial potential? And that's quite difficult to judge but we're looking for some evidence of behaviour which would lead us to think that. And probably the most difficult of all to decide is do I think they would fit into the Company's fairly earthy environment? (Industrial Holding Company)

Acceptability has always been an important criteria of recruitment (Fevre 1992). Jenkins (1985), for example, has shown how the criteria of acceptability operated to the disadvantage of black job-seekers because they were judged to be a threat to the status of white workers. Their occupational recruitment is part of a status-confirming exercise, both for existing employees and for new recruits, as the following recruiter acknowledged:

When people get to the stage of having an offer from us, what they're looking at is a number of things. They're looking at who else has got offers, what's the level at which this firm is offering, can I see people who are good around me, do I want that? . . . Another thing we're looking at is the chemistry that's given off by people who you may not know have achieved various things but, if you put a room full of students together who've had an offer from us, they almost invariably go away and say, "I like the atmosphere in that place". Now, that's important because atmosphere is part of what they're buying. (Accountancy Partnership)

However, in adaptive models of organization, the question of acceptability has assumed even greater significance, for a number of related reasons. As social control within the organization becomes less centralized and looser, the organization cannot function efficiently unless people are willing to commit themselves and share the same corporate goals (Peters and Waterman 1982). It is unsurprising therefore that some of those we spoke to placed considerable importance on learning the "company way" of doing things, its culture and the companys mission statement. Moreover, if work tasks are organized in teams, then it is essential that one recruits team-players. But being a team-player involves more than being willing to work with others; it also involves others being willing to work alongside new recruits. Hence, it involves acceptability as a colleague, project leader, or as a future boss.

One has to remember that I was recruiting someone at the level immediately below myself so I would have to rely on them to relate well to the managers in the company and to the employees of the company. I guess a key requirement is "Did I believe that these people would be acceptable to those managers?" which is partially "Are they acceptable to me?", but I also have to try and put myself in the shoes of the managers and say "How would those managers react to these people?" (Electrical Engineering)

The importance of acceptability also increases because it corrupts the integrity of the public and private as separate spheres of personal life (Merton 1964). Employees are encouraged to view work as a way of life, rather than as a means of earning a living. Acceptability extends beyond an assessment of how the individual will perform "nine till five". Whether the individual will fit into the social scene with colleagues after working hours becomes an important feature of acceptability in adaptive organizations:

We expect a lot of people, in a sense they have not only to pass the exams and qualify, they've not only to be highly rated, but we expect them to have a pretty active social life and be the person that's organized the departmental bash, taken part in the charity events . . . it's those that are generating energy for others from what they're doing. (Accountancy Partnership).

This analysis of acceptability reveals a major contradiction in the rhetoric and reality of graduate recruitment. As companies emphasize the need for people who are innovative and creative, there is, in fact, less room for mavericks, loners, boffins, or individualists. The whole language of personal and social skills is inextricably part of acquiring the appropriate cultural capital:

Interpersonal skills . . . embraces the whole area of personal presentation, personal style . . . chemistry, people who like working with each other, they often have that extra bond and I think psychologists underplay that. So I would put into personal skills the capacity to relate to others that they might be working with. (Accountancy Partnership)

There is a tendency to go for clones. Naturally you try and pick people you know you can work with. Of necessity they're that sort of ilk. (Public Sector Organization)

I suppose to some extent it's a little bit incestuous in as much as you're trying to select people who you think will fit with your culture and that's in the skills of the interviewer to try and get their views on life and management and personnel work in general and see if it gels with your own way of operating. (Pharmaceuticals)

However, another recruiter observed:

The more I think about it, I think that behind your question is, are we selecting a sort of clone or a particular type of person that fits in? I think it's much more that someone who was a pretty rigid type would be very unlikely to get on. I think it's the opposite. And one of the key things is the ability to work with people from other disciplines, other areas, other countries, and if they've got that, then I think they will survive and thrive in this organization. I think if they've got heavy identity hangups in the sense of their own identity or others' identity, it would be very unlikely that they would be able to come in and thrive in this organization. (Pharmaceuticals)

What these quotations reveal is that the whole question of accept-ability is intimately connected to the recent emphasis on personal and transferable skills within higher education (Bailey 1990). What it high-lights is the increased significance attached to social as well as aca-demic qualifications. It is now as necessary to make the "social" grade as the "academic" grade. Thus, we would suggest that cultural capital is increasingly of *direct*, as well as *indirect* importance through the education system.

Few of those we interviewed were able to provide any information about the social backgrounds, gender or ethnicity of recruits. Almost without exception the recruiters in our study were untroubled by questions about possible inequalities in their recruitment of gradu-ates.[3] However, it was acknowledged that because all candidates have to achieve a higher degree or equivalent from a recognized institution of higher education they were recruiting from a relatively level play-ing field. The educational system had already screened and rejected the bulk of "unsuitable" candidates (Ashton et al. 1990, Bills 1988b). A recognition that educational credentials were a proxy for social differences between students was not sullied by innuendoes about class, gender and racial inequalities in education, given that there were seen to reflect differences in innate drive and capacities exposed in the schooling process. Any under-representation, especially of women or ethnic minorities, was because of a lack of applications from such students, rather than to flaws in recruitment procedures. Such mat-ters were seen as being beyond their jurisdiction, although the attempt to influence the content of university curricula was clearly not.

In the case of women, the lack of suitable applicants was a source of regret to at least one male recruiter:

> Assuming that women are as good as the men, and in a lot of cases they may even be better, then there is a chunk of talent which, because they're not studying the sciences in great numbers, is not available to us in the technical recruitment. Out of the people who apply, it's a very small number of women in the technical side. But we tend to take a higher percentage of the women who apply than of the men who apply – which might say something about the quality of the women at that stage. (Petro-chemicals)

Apart from the usual declaration as an "equal opportunities employ-er", there was also little evidence of action programmes aimed at converting this ideal into a reality. Indeed, one of the recruiters was concerned that a strong emphasis on equal opportunities, when seeking to recruit from the ethnic minorities, could lead to a potential decline in standards:

> I don't think we want to be diverted necessarily [by] lowering our standards just to say we've got the requisite number of equal opportunities. It's very hard to find a mix. (Retail Bank)

The significant advances made by female students in recent years has been achieved through access to higher education, despite their concentration in Faculties of Humanities and Social Science (Crompton and Sanderson 1990; Devine 1992). What is abundantly clear is that without a degree one is not in the race. This was justified by employers on the grounds that they required a high level of general education and because the experience of higher education is viewed as helping to build personal confidence and social fit between the student and prospective colleagues:

> A graduate is more confident. They pick up the . . . company culture more quickly. They're able to relate to people a lot more easily – which is what I've found – compared to a non-graduate. A non-graduate might eventually, well they will eventually learn the same skills, but a graduate going into that position seems to instantly have the communication with outside suppliers to all levels. They don't have a problem talking to an MD of a printing company. I've found that the non-graduates do have problems. (Leisure Group)

The recognition that a graduate qualification is required for a growing number of managerial and professional positions has led to more people deferring entry into the labour market in order to secure a graduate qualification (Department of Employment 1992). There has also been a rapid expansion in the number of postgraduate students on Masters programmes, especially the Masters in Business Administration (MBA). Although the acquisition of an MBA is sold as a ticket to the fast-track, several of the employers we spoke to were sceptical of its value both to the student and the company, primarily because it was seen to give its recipients an inflated view of their own value:

> We've flirted with MBAs from time to time. We have on occasions gone through a process where we have sent existing employees to

become MBAs. We identified people of high potential; we sent them to business school and they got their MBAs. We reacted against MBAs and we're going through our anti-MBA phase at the moment, although we might be coming out of it soon. But we had an unfortunate experience with MBAs. We had bright young people; we sent them off; they got their MBAs; they came back; they had totally inflated expectations. They lasted for two or three years and within three years they'd all gone. I'm talking about six or seven of them. It was an enormous investment and we got very little benefit out of it. So because we got our fingers burnt on that it's going to take a while for us to go back into it. (Industrial Manufacturer)

From the employers point of view, this increase in the pool of potential recruits has eased employer fears of a massive shortage of graduate labour prevalent in the late 1980s. However, in the context of economic recession in the early 1990s, the market has been flooded. This has presented recruiters with an almost impossible task of selecting a small proportion of applicants for interview on a rational and fair basis. In such circumstances, the rumour among students that you should send your application in a white envelope because those in a brown envelope are immediately rejected on grounds of poor presentation is not without an element of truth.

This recession has put a lot of the best new practices on the back burner. If you have 200 applications on your desk and half an hour to sort out a short-list, you're going to apply some criteria, and you rule out everybody who has handwritten their application – well, one hopes you don't do that. But it's very difficult so you have to apply some kind of criteria. And you look at the person's specification and that's what we hope people will base their decisions on. (Metropolitan Council)

In reality, some graduates are more equal than others. The hierarchy of universities identified by students was also shared by the recruiters we interviewed, although some were keen to deny that they were influenced by the aura of Oxbridge. However, the hierarchy they adopted when discussing their recruitment strategies varied according to the vacancies to be filled. This hierarchy did not always amount to Oxbridge, the civic universities and the rest; it was more finely calibrated. Some of the new universities were highly regarded by employers, where they were seeking to recruit from courses which had been tailored to their particular requirements; for instance, in the retail industry. In many respects it was believed that students from the new universities were better prepared for the concrete realities of working life, given the applied nature of many of their courses, and a number of respondents stated that they were looking more positively on applications from them:

> . . . we've tended in the past to be pretty well geared towards [the established] universities and, in fact, at one time there was almost the Oxbridge type, you know . . . had been to Oxbridge and had done ancient history and things like that which I find totally . . . and we were stuffed full of them. If you looked at the list of applicants, they had done all sorts of things like anthropology and so on and there was almost a view then that it was the level of intellectual thought capacity which was important . . . most of them that we got that way disappeared off again. I think it was foolish but it was in an era when we were maybe more gentlemanly . . . Certainly, at least in the last five years . . . we have said, "Right, for a start engineers and accountants are what we need in quantity". We don't need people who've done ancient history and we don't really need the languages people and so on. So we've become more choosy. But also we've started pulling away very much from the older, more traditional university . . . we've got a lot of companies where they don't need to be Einsteins, as it were. We need good, practical people. We've got some companies of 50 to 60 people where they could become the general manager quite adequately even if they have got – and I don't believe necessarily the belief that because they've done poly they're more limited than [university] graduates. There are often many domestic reasons why they've gone down that route and why they've not gone down the [established] university route. But I don't think that it will necessarily limit them in where their degree goes to. (Industrial Holding Company)

The problem for the new universities is that although they are perceived to be more in tune with the needs of industry, they are not seen to be able to attract the same calibre of students as attended the established universities:

> I think there are a number of polytechnics who, for whatever reason, offer places to less able students and even though in many cases

polytechnic degrees provide students with relevant skills for business, and therefore they are employable, at the end of the day some of them are still disadvantaged because of their relative incapacity. (Information Technology)

I would say that, as a generalization, which is always dangerous but the graduate university produces is a more polished, confident, able-to-deal-with-group-situations . . . and I think that you could, in sitting at the back of a room, distinguish the university product from the polytechnic product, from polish, poise and confidence, without being snobby or nasty about it. (Industrial Holding Company)

There is a perception that there is a difference, but I think it's a bit elitist to say that some of the universities seem to produce better all-round people. I think it's just the fact that the polytechnics are young and new and we've just got to give them time. There's still a certain snobbishness about going to a good university as opposed to going to your local polytechnic. They've just got to work on their image and make sure that they're getting a share of really good, above-average students . . . Some of my colleagues would say that there is a difference and it's not so much in the product that's coming out as the product that's gone in that's coming out. (Public Sector Organization)

Hence, regardless how hard the new universities try to respond to the demands of employers, for "fast track" graduate recruitment programmes, where the potential for personal development is at a premium, the established universities are at an advantage. The unification of the higher ducation system is unlikely to overcome this problem, given that a hierarchy of institutions will remain, based on the level of entry requirements which are interpreted by employers as a reflection of the calibre of student at a particular university or following specific programmes of study. In sum, existing social inequalities in access to higher education will continue to play a decisive rôle in determining who will become selected for highly paid and high status occupations. The shift towards adaptive and flatter models of organization will reinforce the importance of credentials because the opportunity for upward mobility within companies is severely constrained by the disappearance of large numbers of supervisory and middle managerial positions.

The acquisition of a good degree (upper second class or above) from an established university is the best insurance policy a student can have against being excluded during the initial screening process (Tarsh 1990). However, as organizations modify their recruitment criteria to reflect the demands of work in an "adaptive" rather than a "bureaucratic" environment, the possession of academic qualifications tell employers less about what they need to know regarding potential recruits, given that the very concept of a certification of expert knowledge is inextricably linked to the historical tradition of bureaucratic organizations. Academic qualifications, for instance, convey information about the individual's ability and motivation to jump through the appropriate examination hoops, to follow a course of study and to regurgitate the key points under examination conditions, to recognize and defer to the authority of teachers and lecturers. But as the "code of conduct" has become more personalized, "credentials" convey insufficient information for employers to make judgements about candidates in competition for jobs in postbureaucratic forms of organization. The difficulties this creates for employers was widely acknowledged:

> Recruitment is not a science. There's no precise answer to it. When you take somebody in at the age of 25, say, there is no set thing that will say exactly how that persons career will go. There's no firm objective assessment of what somebodys potential is because you don't know what the positions in your organization are going to be in 30 years' time . . . and the people change as well. Some people get off to a slow start and speed up later. Some people get off to a flying start then stop because they get contented with life. Some people get into a rut which they can't get out of. There's a whole gamut of things which happen. I don't really see that you can specify at the beginning exactly what you will get out of people. (Petrochemicals)

> We find no correlation at all between your degree result and how well you get on in this company. Not at all. I wish there were. I would then be able to say, "Unless you've got a 2:1, don't bother". All being good academically says is that you're good academically. It doesn't say anything else . . . I've got this little quotation from Macbeth here which says: "If I could look into the seeds of time and say which grains will grow, etcetera." Would it be that I had that insight! All I

am able to say . . . was "this guy has got managerial potential". And we weren't able to say, "He's fast". We don't have high-flyers or fast-track people. We have all good managerial potential people. (Industrial Holding Company)

The response of employers to these intractable problems in the recruitment process has been to attach increasing importance to the psycho-social features of human "personality", which has far-reaching implications for understanding who gets selected (Herriot 1984). It has led to an extension and deepening of the selection process. It has been extended by a number of organizations to include various forms of pre-selection such as work- placement and sponsorship schemes. The popularity of industry–education links not only derives from a desire to exert more pressure on the latter to tailor courses to meet employers' needs, but also because it offers recruiters a way of overcoming the limitations of established recruitment practices. Sponsorship schemes and work placements offer an invaluable source of information about potential employees, given that "we can see them, and they can see us":

I don't see it as totally impossible or totally unrealistic to suggest that in a couple of years we won't have a final-year milk round. We might recruit everybody through sandwich course placements or through a vacation scheme, as long as we market it. Because you're seeing people who've been motivated enough not to leave it until the last moment to go and look for a job. You've got people who've had a good look at us so if they decide to go forward to the next stage, they've made a very informed choice about that. We've also got more than an initial 30-minute interview with somebody. We've seen them for a week or longer. So I consider that move happening. Depending on what the success of the scheme this year is going to be, we'll see what happens. (Retail Store)

This targeting of recruitment to a limited range of higher educational institutions, and in some cases to specific courses, is justified on the grounds that such methods are cost effective, given that they consistently supply a significant number of good recruits. This networking between universities and employing organizations also extends to the nurturing of "contacts" between new recruits and their friends from university, some of whom may be preparing to enter the labour market:

The fact is that quite a few first-year students will be going back to a friend's 21st, a club dinner, a sports fixture, to see a boyfriend or girlfriend . . . they go and stay with their friends, and their friends say, "Hey, what's life like? What are you doing?" and those comparisons come out. It's a very powerful part of that networking. (Accountancy Partnership)

Recent recruits are often taken back to their university to give a presentation about the company or to help in the initial selection process. Being recommended by someone who already works for the company may not give them preferential treatment but "anyone who recommends somebody normally would be fairly certain that they would expect that person to be a reasonable standard". With greater weight being given to the criteria of acceptability, the use of networking is likely to increase irrespective of the pretensions of recruiters to offer an open, objective and fair system of recruitment. Those students who do not have access to the appropriate networks will find themselves at a disadvantage in the search for desired jobs (Granovetter 1974). This is a trend which could be reinforced as a result of the "marketization" of education, where the middle classes will seek to ensure that their children gain access to the "right" schools and universities, where they will not only secure the necessary credentials, but also rub shoulders with the "right" people and acquire the relevant cultural capital. There is also recent evidence of graduate employers introducing short-term contracts, which will permit them to screen their pool of new graduates before deciding whom to employ on a more permanent basis.[4]

The recruitment process has also been deepened through the use of assessment centres in order to supplement the standard practice of screening application forms and conducting face-to-face interviews (Herriot 1984). As the art of recruitment increasingly depends upon delving into the personalized world of the individual, so the science of recruitment shifts to finding adequate measures of human personality, motivation, and drive:

We're looking for people who have the usual managerial skills. We're looking for people who have leadership qualities, good interpersonal skills. And assessment centres do that rather well. (Industrial Manufacturer)

... we are experimenting with assessment centres because you can't in an interview really test out somebodys organizational ability or how they work in teams, for example, and it's very difficult to do. So we're looking at structuring assessment centres to be able to bring out those qualities so we have more information to make a judgement on. (Petro-chemicals)

This represents the "commodification" of the whole person, as dress, deportment, speech, skiing holidays, hobbies and interests are all incorporated in the creation of a personality package which must be sold in the job market (Fromm 1949). An interrogation of the socio-emotional world of the individual lays bare much of what remained invisible in the recruitment to bureaucratic organizations, where greater emphasis is given to formally certified forms of expert knowledge and "external" behavioural characteristics which exhibit compliance to formal bureaucratic authority. In recruitment to adaptive organizations the private world of the individual becomes a vital source of information. What, in effect, is being assessed is the outward expression of cultural identity and life-style which inevitably reflects social differences in access to middle-class forms of cultural capital:

If a student has quite clearly been saying, "I go home at weekends to watch the telly, or every weekend is spent playing snooker", then one has to ask the question, "What are they contributing; what sorts of energies are they contributing potentially to their colleagues?" . . . I think there's something pretty fundamental in the way that people who make things happen around them are giving you evidence that they can carry on making things happen around them later on. If you look at our managers and our partners, they're stuffed full of people who were themselves the president of [student societies] at their college, or a county tennis player, or a rowing blue, or whatever. (Accountancy Partnership)

I mean, we recruited one girl last year who got a first class honours from Essex, and she really is the archetypal Essex girl that all these jokes are about. And she's so "cor blimey" that we really did think twice about taking her because she was almost inarticulate. But her brain was so good that we swept all that aside and hoped that she would fit. And the sort of comments I'm getting back about how she's fitted in are that she's picked up the job very well but she looks like a sack of potatoes all the time and doesn't give the confidence to the clients who themselves are like us and want people to work with them to be of the same ilk. So we're almost moulding her to our own standard by suggesting she might dress up a bit better. (Public Sector Organization)

We're always looking for something a little different. I think Alex, our MD, has always been quoted as saying "someone who's canoed up the Amazon backwards we'd choose in preference to someone who's just sat and done nothing at university, other than read for a degree". He likes to see somebody who's a bit different. So people that have done Camp America, who've taken a year off to travel around the world, shown a bit of independence, those are the sort of things we look for . . . People who are ambitious tend to be a leader rather than a follower, so you'll find they'll be secretaries of clubs, they'll be captains of football teams, of cricket, or whatever. You're just looking for something that indicates that they won't just sit down and follow people, that they've actually got some gumption, some get-up-and-go. (Leisure Group)

It is never made explicit to candidates that tennis and rowing exhibit energy and contribution, whereas playing snooker does not. They do not admit that girls with a working-class Essex accent, and who are not into "power" dressing, are invariably excluded, irrespective of their academic abilities. Hence, the extension and deepening of the screening process has become highly "personalized", and it is a recognition of this fact which has led many of these recruiters to use assessment centres in an attempt to objectify (and legitimate) their selection process based on the "results" of standardized exercises and tests. However, their claims that they can successfully neutralize the social dimensions of class, gender, race or ethnicity, in the objective pursuit of talent which will fit into their organizations, cannot hide the reality that recruitment into "adaptive" organizations is pregnant with social significance. In bureaucratic organizations, many aspects of the individual's social world could remain invisible to the recruiter because the rules of the game were explicitly understood (Merton 1964, Bernstein 1975). In adaptive organizations, selection criteria for recruiters, as well as for graduates, are more intangible and implicit. Who gets recruited ultimately boils down to a "gut feeling" of mutual compatibility.

You quite often get a gut feeling that, "Yes, this person's the right personality, the right education, everything". (Leisure Group)

I would like in the recruitment process to do a mutual select. Where you have the candidates, the undergraduates, coming in one direction and the employers going in towards them and as each of us passes across each other, there's a mutual play on "What's the style of management", "Is this an organization I feel I'm going to fit and develop in?", "Is this my style of working?" (Accountancy Partnership)

They're all terribly different. They're from the whole range of structures. You might find someone who's got terribly wealthy parents and some who haven't. It doesn't make a difference. There's no standardization there at all. But they're all perfectly normal actually! They're all perfectly nice! I like the graduates. (Leisure Group)

Material capital has always been invested by middle-class parents in an attempt to confer a social advantage to their children in the competition for academic qualifications (Marshall 1920). Through access to the "right" schools and universities, the conversion of material capital into cultural capital was achieved through the acquisition of high status academic credentials. The evidence presented here suggests that the direct purchasing power of cultural capital in the market for jobs has increased. Therefore, despite more working-class students gaining access to higher education, and the aspirations this is likely to engender, they lack the appropriate *cultural capital* necessary to be selected for managerial and professional jobs. The question of cultural capital is interpreted by employers in terms of social and personal skills and this leads them to demand that the higher education system modifies its curricula and teaching methods accordingly. Hence, interpretations of suitability, capability and acceptability are presented as *technical* problem which can be overcome through technical solutions rooted in education and training systems. However, what this clearly ignores is the fact that an adequate understanding of who gets selected is a "social" question which cannot be divorced from broader questions of social and intergenerational inequalities.

We are not arguing that recruiters deliberately exclude the working-class, women or ethnic minority students, or that the jobs in question smack of contemporary sinecure. Such views are far too simplistic. If large bureaucratic organizations in the past could support large numbers of "unproductive" middle and senior managers, they are now subject to the pressures of intense economic competition, as other companies flatten their structures and remove tiers of middle managers and supervisors. The shift towards adaptive paradigms of organization could open up possibilities for talented people from all walks of life. There is, for instance, some evidence that middle-class women are making important advances into managerial and professional positions. Even so, the demand placed on employers to ensure a personal fit between existing employees and new recruits leads to the search for "safe bets" – that is, those graduates who share common social affinities with recruiters and who are perceived to possess the potential to "fit in" to the organization's "ways of doing things". This is a propensity that has been reinforced by increasing competitive pressures and economic recession, which has led employers to minimize the wastage of resources associated with recruiting people who may not complete the training period, despite the rhetoric attached to ideas about creativity, innovation, and equal opportunities:

> I think what has changed a bit is partly recession. I think we've consciously tightened up in the last two or three years, wanting everyone to be a winner. We want everybody to be able to play their part and we're perhaps less inclined at present to take a flyer on people who maybe bright but lacking in personality, or bright personalities but lacking academic background. We want to try and get a bit of both in them. (Accountancy Partnership)

It is in this way that intergenerational class privileges and deprivations reproduce themselves within organizational processes, and hence the occupational order. But once recruited, how do graduates respond to their employing organizations? We address this issue in the next chapter.

Notes

1. See also Offe 1976, Ashton et al. 1990.
2. Although often unstated, recruiters were always thinking about their selection criteria in terms of jobs to be done, and there was little doubt that if you did not come up to scratch "you were out". But the basic 3Rs

plus some familiarity with information technology was assumed, given the demand for a degree qualification. In terms of technical competence, the fact that it was necessary to have a professional qualification (e.g. environmental health, teaching) presupposed a basic level of technical know-how (Brennan and McGeevor 1988).

3. One noticeable exception was an inner city borough council which was reluctant to employ graduates precisely because they were likely to be white and middle-class! Moreover, it is important to recognize that there may be substantial flexibility and hiring criteria over time. On the basis of case studies in six Chicago organizations, Bills (1988a) suggests that:

    Standards can change quite rapidly in the face of labour market shifts, and managers have far more discretion to adjust hiring criteria than to adjust wage rates. This discretion is bounded in that some jobs are formally closed to those without the proper credentials and probably all jobs are subject to some often dimly perceived *floor*. The point is that managerial discretion is an important part of the processes underlying the association between education and occupational placement. (p. 87)

4. In July 1993 the retail chain Marks and Spencer announced that it was offering temporary jobs to 100 graduates in what was reported to be the first such move by a British company. These "temporary" staff where given no guarantee of employment after a year, but "high flyers may be offered posts if there are vacancies" (reported in the *Independent*, 27 July 1993).

145

CHAPTER SEVEN

Graduates in employment: coming to terms with changing corporate realities

In this chapter we consider the extent to which the experiences of work in changing employment conditions are congruent with students' earlier expectations. As yet the changing graduate labour market and student experiences in adaptive organizations have been subject to little empirical investigation, although there have been a number of studies of school leavers and university graduates which have examined the changing nature of the youth labour market (Ashton et al. 1990) and the transition to work in the 1980s (Brennan and McGeevor 1988; Banks 1992). Moreover, most of the existing data tends to be quantitative, derived from large-scale surveys of occupational choice, or alternatively, of the job destinations of those who have recently graduated from institutions of higher education. In our study, we conducted in-depth interviews with those who were currently in employment and who had graduated from our three institutions, in order to ascertain the extent to which earlier expectations about the world of work had been realized. More specifically, we were interested in exploring how the transition to work in the employment conditions of the 1990s leads to either a positive or a negative orientation to the employment relationship. The small number of students re-interviewed (20) clearly makes it impossible to generalize confidently our findings to all those in this study, let alone to the graduate population as a whole. Further research will also need to be conducted in order to establish the extent to which our findings reflect changing corporate realities, given that graduates have previously been found to experience problems in making the transition to economic life (Herriot, 1984). Moreover, the graduates we re-interviewed

146

were among those fortunate enough to find employment, while others are unemployed or in temporary, low-skilled jobs, waiting for labour market conditions to improve. What our empirical evidence does suggest, however, is a widespread disillusionment with the realities of working life.

Despite the dominance of the traditional bureaucratic orientation among the students in this study, those whom we re-interviewed emphasized short-term goals and expressed considerable uncertainty about their longer-term commitment towards careers in their present employing organizations. Hence, there was a sharp contrast between the attitudes of the students we interviewed at university who subscribed to traditional bureaucratic orientations, and those graduates who were in employment. The work experiences of the latter had compelled them to develop far more pragmatic and flexible career perspectives. Generalizing from our data it was clear that the majority were unprepared for the realities of work in the 1990s: namely the more uncertain career prospects of the adaptive organization. What this evidence suggests is that the vast majority of students are not only psychologically ill-prepared for the uncertain market conditions and the changing nature of work in adaptive organizations, but also that many of those who held traditional bureaucratic orientations while at university are the ones who are the least likely to have the necessary "social" as opposed to "academic" qualifications, which, we have suggested, is now increasingly important for gaining access to good jobs. Hence, it is graduates from lower-status IHEs, and of working-class origin, as well as those from the ethnic minorities and women, who will lack the market power to succeed. By contrast, those at university with flexible orientations were not only psychologically better-prepared for the transition to work, but often also possessed the appropriate forms of cultural capital. Such students tend to be of middle-class origin and to have been to the established universities, especially Oxbridge. The changes in the nature of corporate organizations are therefore reinforcing traditional class divisions that continue to be reproduced within a context of the meritocratic ideology of higher education and employing organizations.

Virtually all the graduates we re-interviewed now exhibit a pragmatic approach, whereby their present employers are perceived to offer means of obtaining relevant experience crucial for future occupational survival. They share a common sense of uncertainty and anxiety which, in turn, affects their attitudes towards work and commitment to their employing organizations. Nevertheless, few of them were expecting to leave their present jobs in the immediate future, given the absence of alternative employment, despite their often expressed frustrations and dissatisfactions, which could range from level of salaries and fringe benefits to relations with colleagues and the nature of their work tasks. However, such discontent was generally regarded as the price to be paid for obtaining "valuable" work experience. For some this could take a number of years, for example, for those pursuing careers in law, accounting and other traditional professional occupations, while for others the time periods were much less. As a consequence, work was perceived to be neither a major source of life satisfaction nor of personal identity, in part because it was now considered virtually impossible to pursue a "career" in a planned or coherent manner. Even for those with "traditional bureaucratic" orientations, promotion and organizational advancement would either occur or it would not; certainly, there was little that could be done about it.

Whereas the predominant cultures of large organizations emphasize the importance of personal achievement and success as measured by upward mobility within corporate structures, newly-recruited graduates attach priority to obtaining technical, specialist and personal skills to have the capacity for self-development and personal growth. While corporate leaders expect a high level of organizational commitment from their graduate employees, since they are the pool from which their successors will be selected, graduates perceive their employing organizations as pragmatic vehicles for developing their own personal, occupational and "transferable" skills.

In earlier decades the values and life-styles of *The organization man* (Whyte 1965) seemed to have prevailed. For managers, the pivot of their personal identities and their social networks was their work. It was around this that emotional and psychological energies were invested and, further, in relation to them that personal, leisure and community relationships were subordinated. It was through work that managers developed specific talents and competences in relation to the needs of their own particular employing organizations, since they pursued organizational rather than occupational careers (Nicholson & West 1988). But since their jobs, located within hierarchical and formalized bureaucratic structures, were often precisely delineated and therefore offered limited opportunities for psychological growth and self-development, careers rather than jobs constituted the key sources of personal motivation (Scase & Goffee 1989). In other words, the performance of job tasks only had meaning or significance for managers because they were part and parcel of hierarchical structures of authority that offered careers and hence capacity for personal growth. It was through the offer of careers, therefore, that organizations could obtain the psychological commitment of their managerial staff, which from the employees' point of view required them to subscribe to the appropriate predominant corporate values and beliefs. Consequently, career success, or to put it another way, upward mobility within corporate hierarchies, entailed a process of socialization whereby ambitious employees obtained the attitudes and personal identities congruent with their mentors, sponsors and others responsible for managerial reproduction. Through this means, cultures of trust became the underlying principle of the management process and the context within which personal competences could be exercised. *The organization man* was psychologically and emotionally, as well as materially, bound to the employing organization and as a result, broader aspects of life-style were both subordinated and an expression of this attachment. Often, career pursuit required geographical mobility and, as a consequence, the continuous buying and selling of houses. With promotion came the transfer to another division, profit centre or operating unit and the need to move home, and with this, often the disruption of children's education and their friendship networks. Equally, the partners of managers were incorporated within their spouse's careers, psychologically and sociologically (Finch 1983). They were often compelled to develop vicarious identities – personalities, attitudes and beliefs – derived from their own absorption in their partners' work, jobs and careers. Geographical mobility, of course, reinforced this process since it reduced the opportunities that partners of managers (particularly female partners of male managers) had for developing their own, independent careers and life-styles. They were, instead, ambassadors for their partners and because of this they, intentionally or unintentionally, became inculcated with corporate values and beliefs and so, indirectly, part of the organization.

Although employers in some instances have become more "greedy" in claims upon the greater majority of their managers' and their managers' partners' time, energies and life-styles, this conflicts increasingly with the changing pattern of middle-class gender relations. There are a number of factors that account for this, associated as they are with internal organizational processes and wider societal trends. It is these that are having an impact upon the attitudes of newly-appointed graduates and which enable us to understand why they have come to define the nature of the psychological bond between themselves and their employing organizations. As we discussed in earlier chapters, companies are undergoing large-scale processes of restructuring, such that the nature of the managerial activity is distinctly different from what it was in the postwar decades. The need to be more adaptive to market trends because of greater competitive pressures on profit margins has forced companies to reduce their management overheads. They have, in other words, "de-layered" their bureaucratic hierarchies and as a result, greatly restricted career opportunities. Without hierarchies, there can only be limited possibilities for promotion and, as such, a key source of managerial motivation has been destroyed. In the "adaptive" organization, often fragmented on the basis of decentralized profit centres within which managers are empowered to achieve pre-negotiated production, sales and turnover targets, rewards are distributed on the basis of performance-related payment systems. In other words, the relationship between organization and employee is more contractual and although the performance of job tasks may be psychologically demanding, it does not generate the same level of emotional commitment. The abandonment of bureaucratic structures has proceeded hand-in-hand with the widespread adoption of information technology and management information systems. This has enabled companies to speed up their processes of bureaucratic de-layering and to "down-size" the overall administrative function. The consequent redesign of jobs, performance reviews and most importantly of all, employees greater vulnerability to redundancy and early retirement, is leading to the redefinition of "management" as a relatively insecure occupation. It is the case that not only are there fewer opportunities for *predictable* career progression but also the general security or structure of corporate life is disappearing. Those in managerial positions find that it is necessary to cope with constant uncertainty and ambiguity in all aspects of their work. This ranges from the nature of job tasks, duties and responsibilities, through to patterns of personal relationships and the overall structuring of work activities. Alongside this, there is a fear of redundancy, caused not only by ongoing organizational redesign, but also by corporate failure, merger and acquisition. All these processes, taken together, have led employees to develop a much more pragmatic approach towards their employing organizations and to curtail the extent to which they are prepared to invest psychological and emotional input into their jobs.

Such redefinitions of the psychological contract are being reinforced by broader societal changes which are having ramifications for the lifestyles and personal relationships of managers. In the past, their structured certainty within employment was reinforced by personal and domestic relations. Male managers, both young and old, could assume the support of their partners in career pursuit. In fulfilling this rôle, wives could be relied upon to "manage" the domestic sphere to free their husbands to throw their energies wholeheartedly into their work. In this way, the corporate career was underwritten by a high degree of material, emotional and psychological permanence. This, of course, is no longer the case; not only are employment relations more temporary and uncertain, but so too are personal relationships. It is now more likely that male partners will be living with women who, themselves, wish to develop their talents and skills within corporate-based work settings. They too will have technical and expert qualifications upon which they hope to establish personal identities that are separate from those of their male partners and the domestic sphere. No longer are they prepared to accept vicariousness and to fulfil solely and essentially support rôles to their male partners. Equally, their perceptions of the domestic sphere are such that partners emphasize the desirability of shared responsibilities in relation to child rearing and other household activities (Beck 1992). Each partner, in negotiation with the other, delineates the division of domestic labour and the appropriate "balance" between home- and work-related activities. Accordingly, each will feel subject to conflicting pressures from these separate spheres of their lives and endeavour to negotiate compromise solutions. An outcome of all this is that whereas in the past, male partners' work dictated the support functions of the domestic sphere, this is no longer the case. Instead, both partners, in separating their work- and home-based identities, establish psychological contracts with their employing organizations so that sharp distinctions are drawn between home and work. The domestic sphere is constituted as an area of "alternative reality", which compensates for the "greedy" pressures of large organizations and within which "independent" identities can be established and acted out (Giddens 1991).

All this creates new demands for those who are engaged in managerial work. No longer can they take for granted a permanent reality of domesticity; instead, this has to be continuously established through negotiation between partners. Accordingly, personal relationships are more prone to break down, especially when each partner has the means for independent survival through their separate participation in the labour market. For this reason, these relationships cannot be neglected or taken for granted and as a consequence, psychological investments in employment – bearing in mind that these are also increasingly transitory – must be carefully constrained and managed. Work has become part of an holistic life-style, according to which priorities and compromises must constantly be negotiated.

There are, then, a number of reasons why younger managers are adopting a more pragmatic orientation to their employing organizations. Because of various internal organizational processes and wider social change they are more inclined to construct sharp divisions between home and work and to define the latter as a means of obtaining desirable rewards. Money is obviously important to newly-appointed graduates, but gaining "experience" and relevant labour market skills are equally so. This is not to suggest that *all* corporate managers will develop and sustain "flexible" orientations as a result of their work experiences; some are highly committed to their employing organizations and perceive them to offer contexts for self-development and personal growth, as with the traditional bureaucratic orientation. In our own study, few of the respondents who were at work had faith in the career strategies which the majority of the undergraduates assumed would be available to them. There were some differences between the graduates of the three institutions – not surprisingly, those from Oxbridge were more optimistic about career chances than the others. But, overall, career expectations had been dampened by their initial employment experiences. Nevertheless, it was a crucial part of their everyday lives which had to be negotiated alongside other concerns, of which relationships with present or future partners were high on the agenda.

Some examples of how recently recruited graduates locate work within their general life-styles are illustrated by the following:

[Work] well it's not the most important thing, [although] when I'm at work it pretty well is. I tend to devote all my time and all my mental attention to my work when I'm at work really. I've been struggling through the last few months to bring home less work because it was interfering, it was taking up too much of the weekends and too much of the evenings and I'm sure that it will get better next year. I know that it's difficult to find a job that you enjoy and so I certainly value that. But I'd be much more concerned about something that went wrong at home than something that went wrong at work really. (Male, Oxbridge)

My personal relationships are terribly important to me and to say that work takes second place to these is true on a broad level but on a day-to-day basis it isn't necessarily like that. I mean there are times clearly when work is, there's a crisis on but that doesn't mean that globally work is more important than personal relationships. I'm in no way a workaholic. I'm capable of turning around and saying "I've got enough work to do", you know, "I'm not going to take this extra job". If as a result of a personal relationship that was terribly important to me, I was asked to move out to . . . I suppose it inevitably involves a compromise doesn't it? If I was in a relationship, I'm not at the moment, but if I had a partner and he wanted to make a career move in a particular direction, my career would definitely be part of that discussion. I would want to work out my career issues in the context of my relationship. I'm not someone, I don't think, who will ever give up my career totally in order to be a purely domestic person. That's not me, but if it was a choice between a relationship and a career, I would make adjustments in the career before I would make adjustments in the relationship. (Female, Oxbridge)

I think I would be very careful in a possible partner, not to pick up somebody who has a different view to me. I mean, I would hate to be in a situation where suddenly, you know, my husband or husband-to-be turns round and says something shocking like, you know, "When you get pregnant you will give up your job won't you?" Or somebody else who is in a job which needs the traditional back-up, you know, the entertaining wife, and who has to go on business trips and all that sort of stuff. But I don't think I've got much in common with that kind of person anyway. I mean I've met plenty of them. No, I've, never, never really considered that I would end up with someone like that. (Female, Home Counties)

My personal life has got to come first really. I know you spend most time at work but I think that's wrong really. I think you should have a life outside work – that's what makes you an interesting person. But all those activities, even just going on holidays, cost money. When you're at work you put in 100 per cent but it's nine-to-five and then end of story. I'm not saying I don't think of ideas when I'm not at work but I try not to think of them too often. (Male, Inner City)

Work has a rôle within the context of personal relations, which are considered to be of greater importance – a sharp contrast to the picture of *The organization man* as depicted in the management literature of the 1960s and 1970s. But also, we would suggest, this is a frame of mind which corporate leaders try to change through putting newly-recruited graduates on management development programmes, induction courses and culture-building schemes. From an alternative perspective, however, it could be that these graduates have formulated a more rational approach to personal wellbeing. It would hardly be sensible to direct *all* of ones energies into work and to subordinate all other aspects of life to it in view of the uncertainties associated with present-day corporate realities. It is clearly more sensible to locate personal psyches mainly *outside* the world of work so that the individual personality and identity is less vulnerable to potential organizational threats (Beck 1992).

How do recently-recruited graduates make sense of contemporary changing corporate realities? From our interviews, it would seem they have very limited understanding of the direction of organizational change and the ways in which this is likely to affect the need for particular employee competences. In many ways this is to be expected, given the recent and ongoing nature of these changes. What is evident from our interviews however, is that respondents no longer expect to have long-term careers, but they do recognize the need to possess a range of personal and transferable skills generally considered to be appropriate for employment in organizations structured according to adaptive paradigms. Some of the following comments illustrate such attitudes:

I wouldn't move to another company in this group. I want to move outside the structure. I'll see how it goes. I think at some point or other I've got to start moving up the scale in whatever I do. I don't think it's too good to stay near the bottom or even in the middle when you're getting older. I think you've got to cover all the angles and make yourself as marketable as possible. Of course, other people are talking about doing the same things, but I'll have to put it into action. (Male, Inner City)

I'll do this job for about another year because I think the actual job will be done by then because it's a new subsidiary that's been put together with six companies that we've recently bought and, therefore, there's a lot of work to do. I think in about a year's time they won't need a business development manager and I accept that. But they would want to move me internally and I may or may not accept that move. If I don't, I would go to business school. (Male, Oxbridge)

I don't necessarily plan to stay in one firm for a long time. Really I would like to get, again, different experience, ideally what I would like to do is run my own business or whatever, but for that, obviously, you need to know what you are doing and you need a good idea. My next step would be to get a job in industry – what sort of industry I haven't really decided. But I would be looking for something in the manufacturing business rather than the retail sort of business. That's more a gut feeling than any sort of specific plan or anything. (Male, Oxbridge)

I saw an advertisement in the *Richmond and Twickenham Times* for this job and thought "Well, that sounds like fun" and went along for the interview, ended up lying through my teeth, making it through to the second interview and being chosen. I kept it all very quiet for about, you know, six weeks and then, in fact, I realized, it suddenly dawned on me one day that I was very much enjoying the atmosphere I was working in and that there were prospects within this area, within the fitness industry and so I decided to stay, which is quite bizarre, but then I think it happens to a lot of people. I have had a career shift before I had even started one, if you like. (Female, Home Counties)

These orientations are essentially pragmatic and underwritten by feelings that all work experiences are likely to be short-term and shrouded in uncertainty and change. Employing organizations are generally perceived to be non-meritocratic, with personal career paths often shaped by patronage and personal sponsorship. Hence, considerable importance is given to cultivating personal networks. There is a recognition that these are manipulated by senior managers who are able to dictate appropriate personal managerial styles, and the criteria of personal effectiveness that, in the final analysis, determine the recruitment and promotion process. These factors are in sharp contrast to the explicitly meritocratic cultures of IHEs and, as such, generated feelings of cynicism and, occasionally, outright antagonism among the recently-recruited graduates we interviewed. Needless to say, the Oxbridge graduates were seen to be in an advantaged position within these corporate processes by comparison with those who had graduated from the two other institutions. The following illustrates these points:

> There's quite a heavy Oxbridge contingent but it's changing. I mean I'm not sure how many of us were Oxbridge in our intake. I don't know, between 20 and 25 per cent, or perhaps not as high as that. They're a very nice bunch of people, I mean as a whole. I feel that they're all very much my sort of people. How much that is also because they were my sort of people at Oxbridge I don't know, do you know what I mean? They're nice people, they are intelligent, they are quietly driven, they want to get a good job done. They're committed and this is very broadly generalising, but at the same time they're pleasant people, they've got a sense of humour, there's a good sense of humour here. They enjoy their work. They all play hard, they all, you know, have lots of other interests as well. Pretty English. I mean, you know, there are some foreigners here, which is great. There's some Australians, New Zealanders and Canadians. I suppose the greatest contrast, in a way, with some other firms is a label of being very arrogant. These people aren't arrogant, not personally arrogant. They're self-confident, certainly, but they're not arrogant. They're also not the sort of wide red braces brigade, you know what I mean, they're not wide boys in any way. I think it probably does help [coming from Oxbridge]. I mean there's no doubt in my mind that having an Oxbridge degree helped and also, I mean, the fact that in my second year I got a first and that helped enormously. But at the same time my name was known in the City anyway, so that was another factor which is a bit unusual. But I do think, I mean last week they [the firm] had a sort of a social in Oxford and a social in Cambridge so that they could try and do some more

recruiting, and I think that does, no doubt, continue, no question. (Female, Oxbridge)

This sums up succinctly the ways in which the internal dynamics of many organizations – based upon personal networks, patterns of mutual acceptability, and implicit but understood shared meanings and values – constitute cultural barriers that mitigate against the recruitment and career advancement of those lacking the necessary but inevitably intangible qualities of charismatic personality. In such circumstances, an Oxbridge background is almost imperative because it is, by definition, linked to particular and preferred personal attributes, values, and patterns of conduct. For others, lacking such a background, it is necessary to be sponsored and coached so that such personal qualities can be acquired. Indeed, graduate training programmes in many organizations are as much to do with the socialization of recruits and the indoctrination of key values as they are with the acquisition of technical and functionally-specialist skills. Of course, graduates from the other two institutions co-operating in our study are well aware of this, as the following graduates explained:

Many managers have either worked their way up and become what they would perceive as relatively middle class, or come straight in anyway from other senior management positions in other industries. If one is going to have to work with and relate to these people, it obviously is of benefit to have a similar social background. Just so that you can talk to them freely with the same common, or a commonality of experience, as part of a club. It wouldn't do any good to talk with a working-class accent. (Male, Home Counties)

It is also a case of if your face fits. I think they decide if you're going to fit into the organization from your voice and the way you dress and your accent. I think in this organization you've got to stand up and express your ideas. The person who had the job I'm in now was very quiet and very plodding and worked very hard but it took her a long time to get promoted. It's no good concentrating on the plodding everyday jobs. You've got to do the jobs that get you noticed. (Female, Inner City)

I asked them how many they had taken on from the new universities and it was obvious they'd never had any before and they were interviewing a few token ones from new universities. That was my

157

impression anyway. I mean everybody knows most firms will go for Oxbridge graduates if they can get them. I think it's a case of whether your face fits or not. (Female, Inner City)

I think you've got to be very much self-driven. You've got to be able to blow your own trumpet and you have to work the system and look good all the time and, like, stay one step ahead of the game all the time. So that they can trust you and you can take decisions, so they think, "Oh, this guy is a good little boy." It's a game really and a lot of it is luck. There's no actual overt way of portraying this but I believe that if I was in a position to go up into the echelons within the company I think I would find it really difficult. There would be a few obstacles put up in my way or to slow me down. I've looked at the way they promote people in the Company and a lot of them are wimps really, who've made a load of mistakes. And I think they've promoted them because it doesn't threaten them. But it's complex; there's other things that can happen as well – if you're too good at your job they can just leave you there, 'cos it's good for them. I don't know if all companies are like that but certainly this one is. (Male, Inner City)

Not surprisingly, such cynicism, or at least scepticism, affects the longer-term aspirations of recently-recruited graduates. Because they are of the opinion that all large employing organizations are much the same – with opportunities and rewards strictly "managed" within "core" interpersonal networks and cultural processes – some are attracted by the appeal of entrepreneurship and small business start-up. For them, establishing a business offers the possibilities for obtaining a greater degree of personal independence whereby their life chances will not be controlled by the arbitrary and discretionary judgements of others. It is this, rather than the possibilities of enhanced financial rewards that constitutes the attraction of entrepreneurship. Business start up, therefore, for these young graduate employees usually has little to do with their commitment to "enterprise" values popularly associated with Thatcherism. On the contrary, it is more likely to be an expression of their resentment towards the managerial control of large organizations structured, as these are perceived to be, upon intangible and non-meritocratic criteria of selection and promotion. Some of them resent the relative absence of explicit and formal criteria of personal performance which can reinforce their own dependency upon the discretionary judgements of organizational leaders, and, often more importantly, their immediate bosses. The "enterprising" graduates, then, are attracted to business start-up to avoid these control relations and to escape the growing uncertainties of organizational life. They seek alternative careers for personal development under circumstances that enable them to use more fully their personal talents and skills. Among those we interviewed in employment, none of them who had graduated from Oxbridge had considered business start-up. Generally, they had little need to, not only because of the "fit" that existed between their own psychological predispositions and the dominant cultural values and opportunity/promotion processes of their employing organizations, but also as a result of their market power derived from their superior cultural capital. It was, by contrast, among the graduates of the other institutions that entrepreneurship had its appeal. This, it should be stressed, was more rhetorical than real; the attraction was the expression of an "idealized alternative" rather than as a practical and seriously-considered possibility. None of those we interviewed had attended a business start-up course, or indicated evidence that they had the available resources necessary to start their own businesses:

> Everybody's always talking about starting up their own businesses, but I don't know. I'm supposed to be working with somebody now and I've got to get down to it. I tried before actually, and we actually built the device. It was a burglar alarm – but I went back to college and it just sort of faded away, which was a pity really because I think it would've made a bit of money. I would like to work for a small company or be involved in a small company, because you can do so many different things. I could do quite a good job influencing people to buy things if the products good. I'd rather be the director of a small company than be in somewhere like GEC because they're not like Alan Sugar, Anita Roddick and Richard Branson. Those sort of people keep in touch with what's going on, on the shopfloor. But our lot, they've got their mobile phones and Jags, house in the country and they think they're sitting pretty. (Male, Inner City)

I have been looking more in terms of being able, once I'd learnt enough, to develop my own work environment. A few of us were going to start a computing co-operative, developing software . . . I won't work my way up here because for one thing there's very few opportunities. And the plan for the co-operative is on hold, and since the Tories have got back in, I think it will be on hold for a long time – there's so many small businesses going down; it's not the right time. (Female, Inner City)

Large organizations, then, are often perceived by their newly-recruited graduates as essentially non-meritocratic; particularly by contrast to the cultures of the institutions to which they belonged as students. Clearly, the contemporary popularity of adaptive paradigms of organization design, because of their alleged capabilities for generating entrepreneurial, creative and risk-taking behaviour, can backfire. This is certainly the case for many graduates, instilled as they are with values of competence, expertise and, perhaps most important of all, notions of equity and fairness. They develop attitudes of resentment and cynicism when such features are perceived to be absent, as is often the case within their own employing organizations. Such views become even more pronounced when issues of gender and race are considered.

All the female graduates we re-interviewed believed that their gender had placed them at a disadvantage when compared to their male colleagues, in terms of the opportunities that were available within their employing organizations. Some of the reasons for this are to do with the ways in which "networks" within organizations "manage" the promotion processes. Since such networks are managed in the main by older white men who determine criteria of personal effectiveness, it is not surprising that highly-qualified younger women and ethnic-minority graduates are seen by them to be "high-risk", if only by virtue of being a potential "threat" to the established patriarchal order of things. Of course, within organizations it is not articulated in this way; instead, within different work settings, the explicit criteria for "female exclusion" form around issues of child-bearing and personal ability:

I think they're interested in your marital, family plans, obviously because of the maternity aspects. It hasn't become an issue with me because of the two-year contract. But I think if when it comes to talking about a longer-term contract, or being taken on permanently, either by this firm or another one, I'm led to believe that it's one of the first questions that's asked. (Female, Home Counties)

In any interview you have to try and find a point of personal contact so that you can bring yourself out, or be brought out by the interviewer. I suppose in some respects that mutual interests are inevitable, if you know what I mean. They have a very good female policy and there are lots of women joining and women are treated very well. Well, um, there's a question mark in my mind. I think that women are pushed harder than some of the men. I don't know whether that's because they're more capable or whether it's because they've got more to prove. I think I would have to know the people concerned a little bit better to be able to assess that. But I do get a feeling of women being pushed a bit harder than some of the men. I think there are certainly some who find it difficult to deal with women on a working level, you know, they find it difficult to look them straight in the face, if you know what I mean. Those whose wives, for example, are at home looking after five children, and you get this sort of, there are women who are wives and women who work, and the only real women are the women who are wives. That exists, but I think it varies, I think it depends a great deal on what kind of women they've had exposure to and who their wives are. I think some women are much more driven than men, but I also think there's an element of testing out the women. You know, "You're here, you say you're as good as we are, you prove it". (Female, Oxbridge)

Even those women who could be seen to possess the personal qualities most likely to be considered "acceptable" by organizational leaders experience barriers to their career progression. If women who are white, from middle-class backgrounds and have been educated at Oxbridge encounter difficulties, then it is unlikely that working-class women or ethnic minorities who have attended the less prestigious established or new universities will do better. They are even more likely to lack the perceived qualities seen to be illustrative of leadership potential and to be condemned therefore to, at best, the middle echelons of the management process. It is little wonder that more women in Britain in the 1990s have abandoned their jobs in large organizations and set up their own small businesses (Davidson & Cooper 1992). Despite the obstacles of raising finance and achieving trading viability, they are able to avoid the psychologically damaging

161

experiences associated with working in patriarchal organizational cultures and the invidious "controls" exercised over them by their male colleagues.

In this chapter we have reviewed some of the corporate realities of recently-recruited university graduates. It is a picture that offers little comfort to those who expect de-bureaucratized, de-layered organizations to generate greater entrepreneurial attitudes among their better-educated employees. The abandonment of hierarchical structures and a shift away from bureaucratic paradigms seems to have restricted, rather than extended, the level of organizational commitment that graduates are likely to exhibit. The flattening of structures has, of course, reduced the opportunities for career paths and, associated with this, the possibilities for long-term planning in relation to careers and personal life-styles. Instead of instilling a greater propensity to take risks and to be highly-committed corporate performers, there is a tendency for the reverse to occur. Newly-recruited graduates are responding to the uncertainties and insecurities of their jobs by with-holding their psychological engagement. However, because of the broader economic recession, they are not resigning their jobs. Without being embedded within clearly-defined career structures, their jobs are less meaningful, so that, unlike their predecessors described in *The organization man*, their orientations to their employers are pragmatic (in order to gain experience) and short-term. An outcome of this is the performance of tasks according to *satisfying* rather than *optimising* criteria – quite the reverse of what is expected of behaviour within "adaptive" forms of organization. This, in turn, leads us to a further conclusion; that attempts to breakdown bureaucratic structures are leading to a re-emphasis upon a wide range of invidious and intangible criteria within the promotion and reward systems of organizations (Bennis 1972). Without the measurable "yardsticks" of the explicit kind found within more formalized structures, personal discretion through sponsorship and patronage becomes more apparent (Smith 1989). This, in turn, is leading to a growing division among the more highly educated. Although they may be more or less equal in terms of technical, specialist and professional competences, some are more favoured than others through their possession of cultural capital and interpersonal skills, which are compatible to the prominent values of senior management within essentially patriarchal organizational cultures. It is this that generates for "excluded" graduates feelings of inequity and which also contributes to the reproduction of class, gender and ethnic divisions within the corporate structures of Britain in the 1990s.

CHAPTER EIGHT

Mass higher education and
the collapse of bureaucratic work?

As organizations move from bureaucratic to adaptive models of organization, managers, administrators and professionals need to be more flexible, creative, innovative and socially skilled. Protagonists of this view can point to the rapid expansion of higher education in Britain as testimony to a general upgrading of human resources. We have already noted that by the end of the 20th century, approximately one-third of 18 to 21-year-olds can expect to be in some form of higher education, along with a growing number of mature students.[1] This has led Ball (1990) to suggest that the economic compulsion of enlightened self-interest has become so compelling that there is now "a commonality of interest between those who want to run effective businesses and those who want to meet the needs of the underprivileged in our society".[2]

The changing relationship between education and occupational structure not only derives its importance as a question of social justice, but equally as a question about national economic competitiveness (Stephens 1989). In a number of influential reports, for instance, the importance of a nations human resources to its future economic prosperity has been clearly recognized (CBI 1989, Porter 1990). Moreover, the education and selection of those who will become the future business leaders and corporate managers has gained added significance. However, Collins (1979) claimed that large numbers of managerial and professional jobs in corporate bureaucracies are little more than contemporary sinecures for the middle classes, where the productivity of the recruits matters little so long as they do not "rock the boat". Whatever the substance of Collins' claim, the exclusion of talented and highly motivated individuals who may not conform to the middle-class, white, male stereotype, is likely to prove far more damaging in the context of intensive international economic competition.[3]

The purpose of this book has been to investigate the changing relationship between higher education and the intergenerational reproduction of class inequalities in light of the "adaptive" paradigm and educational reform. Although our conclusions must remain tentative, they contradict the celebratory rhetoric of widening access, opportunity and social mobility harboured in the official discourse on educational expansion and labour market flexibility. In this conclusion we extend the key elements of our argument in order to show how the wastage of talent, which has been an endemic feature of British society throughout the 20th century, shows little sign of being eradicated in economic circumstances which it can ill-afford, and political circumstances which expose an education system and a labour market that continues to favour higher socio-economic groups.

In Chapter 2 we identified two competing theories that offer explanations of the relationship between educational and occupational stratification. We showed that from a technocratic point of view the move towards a mass system of higher education is understood as an inevitable consequence of post-industrial development, reflecting its pivotal rôle in the socialization and selection of a growing army of skilled technicians, managers and professionals (Clark 1962, Perkin 1989). In these terms, the labour market acts as a matching device, uniting a hierarchy of qualified talent with a hierarchy of skilled occupations. Alternatively, social exclusion theory asserts that although there has been a significant expansion of higher education during the 20th century, it cannot be explained in terms of an increased demand for a skilled workforce.[4] Rather, the technocratic explanation is seen to serve little more than an ideological justification for professional groups, who engage in the intensive and extensive "examination" of potental entrants in order to restrict the numbers gaining access to their ranks. Therefore, Collins (1979) argues that the relationship between higher education and occupation stratification should not be seen to reflect the allocation of human expertise to appropriate slots in the occupational structure, but as a power struggle for scarce credentials, used for the purposes of excluding less powerful groups from gaining access to professional enclaves offering high status and material rewards.[5] In our attempt to understand the changing relationship between education and occupational stratification, both these approaches are problematic, because they have been linked to alternative visions of work and social structure in advanced capitalist societies.[6] Technocratic theory has been associated with "embourgeoisement" and a shift to a "professional" society, given its focus on the upgrading of occupational skills, whereas a lack of such evidence (or evidence of de-skilling) has been related to arguments about enduring class divisions and the proletarianization of white-collar workers (Braverman 1974).

This link between credentials, skills and class structure has become more of a problem in a context of rapid economic change. The use of "skill" or "credentials" as a proxy for occupational status, rewards, security, career prospects and life chances is increasingly untenable. The ticket obtained on leaving school or university is no longer for a life journey (Marshall 1963, 113). Similarly, few of those in highly-paid and prestigious occupations can be guaranteed long tenure or career advancement as organizations in the private sector "down-size", merge, restructure or are taken-over, and those in the public sector are subject to "market" competition through competitive tendering, contracting out, or being sold off. Therefore, an increase in the demand for knowledge workers does not mean that a larger number of employees will make "careers" rather than hold "jobs" (Hughes 1958) because the underlying assumptions about employment contracts, conditions and relations in postwar western capitalist societies no longer hold with the demise of bureaucratic work.[7] Occupational insecurity previously associated with semi-skilled and unskilled workers now characterizes *all* jobs. This has not occurred primarily as a result of de-skilling, but due to changing organizational imperatives, which in Britain has often meant "down-sizing" as a means of cost cutting rather than as an attempt to create a learning organization (Zuboff 1989). Moreover, the increasing tendency for adaptive organizations to distinguish between strategic "core" employees and contract, peripheral and support workers, also suggests that a hierarchy of "skills" and "occupations" cannot be juxtaposed, as has been the convention.[8] The de-layering of organizational bureaucracy serves in many instances to widen the division between the strategic core of senior managerial personnel and the remainder of the workforce. Hence the decoupling of the bureaucratic routes into the upper tiers of the hierarchy places even greater emphasis on access to initial "fast track" training programmes in order to climb truncated corporate career ladders and to obtain a "value added" curriculum vitae.

The implications of these changes are being reflected in the process of graduate recruitment where a hierarchy of jobs for which a graduate qualification is necessary will emerge, with a growing polarization between a fast-track providing access to senior managerial positions, and the rest. As a recruiter we interviewed made clear:

> I think the way things are developing at the moment, with the reduction in the number of vacancies . . . and . . . an increasing population coming out of higher education, you're going to get different levels of intake . . . I think you're going to see more and more firms looking at this because there is increasing access into higher education so you're going to have less and less people going to become available at GCSE and A level, therefore there will be a higher population coming out and available at graduate level. But companies will not necessarily be wanting to pay the higher, fast-track salaries for those people. Therefore they will be coming and saying, "We have the jobs but they're not on the fast-track level . . . and that's what you're being considered for".

Therefore, although the bond between education and occupational stratification has been tightened because employers are demanding graduate qualifications for a growing number of jobs, that between graduate employment and extensive career opportunities has been ruptured. So, the changing relationship between education and occupational stratification has undermined the conventional career paths of the higher educated, although a majority of students we interviewed remained locked into the idea of future bureaucratic careers. Moreover, the experiences of those graduates we interviewed who were in employment suggest that the rhetoric of the adaptive organization may hide a reality of dissatisfaction, frustration, and stress which is leading some at least to maintain a division between their public "work life" and private "personal life" as a coping strategy (see also Scase & Goffee 1989). In a labour market where there are few alternatives available, many graduate employees may stay in their present jobs in the hope of better things to come. The longer term-implications of such problems, coupled with the high proportion of unemployed and underemployed graduates, are vital research questions, not only for our understanding of the changing pattern of education, occupational stratification and class divisions, but because the economic prosperity of the nation is seen to depend upon the exploitation of the insights, knowledge and energies of the more highly educated.

These changes have served to heighten the competition for credentials which offer opportunities for fast-track graduate training programmes at a time when more students are gaining access to higher education. The expansion of HE has led to a rapid increase in the number of labour market entrants with graduate level qualifications. However, given that the whole purpose of academic credentials in the job market is to provide employers with a convenient and cheap means of screening candidates, employers are likely to lift their entry requirements from degree to masters level qualifications and, in turn, to recruit graduates for jobs which previously did not require a university education. Hence the

> excess of apparently qualified candidates induces an intensification of job screening that has the effect of lengthening the obstacle course of education and favouring those best able to sustain a longer or more costly race. These are the well off and the well connected. (Hirsch 1977, 50)

Moreover, because degree holders stand "relative" to one another on a hierarchy of social worth, as the number of degree holders increases, so the social distance between graduates becomes more important. Employers will become increasingly discerning about the status of the credentials as well as the personal qualities of the individuals possessing them. As graduate qualifications become more common, some graduates will become even more equal than others. A degree from Oxbridge or a civic university will carry more "weight" than one from a new university. It is also likely that organizations offering fast-track training programmes will intensify their targeting of recruits at institutions offering "quality assurance". This will come as no surprise to the students in this study, who were well aware of where they stood within the hierarchy of academic worth, although it was sometimes recognized as reflecting social differences rather than being the outcome of a meritocratic race. Moreover, an increasing differentiation between universities not only reflects the demands of students and employers, but also the vested interests of university staff

(Bourdieu 1988). With the collapse of the binary system of universities and polytechnics, and significant changes to the way universities are funded, the established universities have already shown a keen interest in maintaining status differentials and to repel government attacks on their *modus operandi*. In an expansion programme without adequate financial resources such tactics have been justified in order to maintain academic standards.[9] Within a unified system of university education there has already been an increased concentration of research funds going to the elite institutions.[10] The maintenance of academic standards is also being used to legitimate the introduction of top-up fees for students, because the price the government is willing to pay for each student is no longer sufficient to maintain a high quality of teaching. These arguments have not only led to a distinction between teaching and research universities (which looks suspiciously like the old binary division, but with some blurring at the edges), but also to an increasing likelihood that some of the elite institutions will introduce top-up fees, where middle-class students will be expected to "pay for their privilege".[11]

The financial burden increasingly involved in studying for a degree because of the declining value of state-funded grants to undergraduate students is reflected in the increasing proportion of students failing to complete their studies. In 1991, 13.1 per cent of students from the established universities either dropped out or switched courses; in the new universities the comparable figure was 15.3 per cent. The president of the National Union of Students, Lorna Fitzsimons, suggests that:

> Students cannot cope with increased financial and academic pressures and the stress of knowing there is a reduced chance of finding a job at the end. Some are taking the easy way out because they are better off on the dole!

The relationship between education, credentials and class divisions has also changed, because employers are placing increasing importance on *social* as well as *academic* qualifications. The possession of advanced academic qualifications was useful to employers in large bureaucratic organizations, not only because of their relative scarcity value in the 1950s and 1960s, but also because this "certified" compliance to bureaucratic authority and control. However, the increased emphasis on charismatic "personal qualities" as opposed to bureaucratic "individual attributes" in adaptive organizations has led employers to supplement the information conveyed by credentials. Employers are making more use of various assessment techniques in order to legitimate their "gut feelings" about the personal qualities of candidates and the use of "compacts" and "scholarships" which bind students and employers more closely together. Such assessments are becoming especially popular among employers in the fields of science and technology, where recruitment problems continue.

However, the rise of mass higher education is unlikely to give lower socio-economic groups access to the fast-track, partly because they are unlikely to display the *social* qualifications that employers covet. This is despite the fact that the new universities have modified their curricula to develop the personal, social and enterprise skills of students, while the elite universities have been conspicuous by their inaction. Indeed, the formal teaching of personal and social skills represents the latest version of "compensatory" education for those who lack the personal qualities which come naturally through the everyday social education within the middle class family and educational settings.

Moreover, in the past twenty years, IHEs have been called upon increasingly to "meet the needs" of industry. These debates have focused on the ways in which IHEs can be reorganized to contribute to the nations economic competitiveness. A key issue that has a direct bearing on the conclusions of this book is the idea that an anti-industrial ideology pervades the whole education system, and that there is a need for a counter-hegemonic assault through the creation of an enterprise culture. However, the overwhelming sense given by the students in this study was of HE as a *status-confirming* activity. The professions dominated responses about preferred employment, and clearly had a profound impact on their choices of university studies, reflected in the perennial problem of attracting students into science and technology. Those planning non-conventional careers were heading for such occupations as management consultancy and the media. The management consultants epitomize the difference between the *entrepreneurial* and the *enterprising*. These students were enterprising in that they were going to draw upon their knowledge, credentials and contacts to move from one company to another, gaining necessary experience and "challenges", which they would later convert into an executive position in a medium-sized or large organization (perhaps even in an industrial organization). There was no way they were going to "get their hands dirty" learning about the nature of an industrial process which could then be used to engage in technological innovation, or turning their knowledge into an entrepreneurial venture. If Schumpeter is right that private empire-building through the deliberate search for technological innovation is the essence of capitalist dynamics (Collins 1986, 113), then the status system of business over the past 200 years has been a key factor in undermining the spirit of enterprise in Britain, and shows little sign of being overturned by ideas of the enterprise culture popularized during the 1980s. *The anti-industrial bias is not a British disease, it is a class disease.* Male working-class youth has traditionally opted for craft apprenticeship in industry (Brown 1987). The point here is that student experience of higher education represents the visible expression of status hierarchies which guide the predilections of parents, students, lecturers *and* employers, it is therefore "impossible to alter institutions without altering that valuation" (Tawney 1982, 10).

Enterprise in the context of late 20th century Britain has not become a source of "creative destruction" in Schumpeters (1976) terms, whereby capitalism constantly renews itself through innovation and change, but rather the creative construction of individualistic work portfolios. A hefty cocktail of western individualism, a cultural climate with the overriding emphasis on self-interest, and continuing economic recession, make a substantial personal commitment to any particular employing company inadvisable in light of corporate restructuring and potential take-over. In this sense, Britain may be suffering from a lack of well educated *intra*preneurs as well as *entre*preneurs. Moreover, the use of graduate entry schemes and fast-tracks for the high-flyers provides a constant reminder to motivated and talented employees who do not have a graduate qualification, that no matter how hard they strive, they are severely disadvantaged in the competition for appointment to most management positions. For those who miss out on the "fast-track", the opportunity to gain promotion by proving ones worth "on the job" is increasingly less of an option.

Fallows argues that we need to distinguish between an entrepreneurial society and a professionalized one:

> an entrepreneurial society is like a game of draw poker, you take a lot of chances because you're rarely dealt a pat hand and you never know exactly what you have to beat. A professionalized society is

more like blackjack, and getting a degree is like being dealt a nineteen. You could try for more, but why?" (Fallows 1985, 64)

In these terms, Britain remains a "professionalized" society despite the importance of education to economic development, and despite the fact that in recent times it is argued that the creation of a market for education is the best way of ensuring that the needs of employers are met (Hague 1991). The reality is that the education system in general, and the market system in particular, undermines the creation of a "risk" society (Beck 1992). A risk society is not only one which is "open" in the sense that status and rôles are not determined on the basis of ascribed characteristics – class, gender, ethnic background and age – but also one which encourages moderate risk-taking, novel insights and activity, as well as individual responsibility.[12]

The overriding conclusion of our analysis is that the changing relationship between education, employment and social class does not represent the creation of a "risk" society in which all individuals are free to use their own efforts, abilities and initiative in order to make something of their lives. Rather, it suggests that success in the education system and the labour market depends upon access to significant financial resources to buy an educational advantage at all levels of the system, from preschool to university. It also depends upon forms of cultural capital which exude social confidence, charisma and compatibility in the competition for superior jobs. As employers create an elite route for those at the top of their graduate intake, although there may be "token" (Kanter 1984) representation from the working-class, ethnic minorities and in most cases a somewhat larger representation of women from middle-class backgrounds, there may be even less room at the top for the sons and daughters of disadvantaged groups than has been the case in the postwar period. Moreover, the collapse of bureaucratic work, high rates of graduate unemployment and the expansion of higher education have served to heighten the perceived "risk" to the social reproduction of middle-class family life. As a result, there is clear evidence of higher socio-economic groups exerting their superior market power in the name of wanting the best for their children (Brown 1990, David 1993).

The middle class has sought to monopolize high-status credentials in order to reduce the risk of downward social mobility and uncertain economic life-chances, both for themselves and for their off-spring.

Moreover, the shift to free market systems of education will not increase the entrepreneurial energies of middle-class students but will increase the potential use of the education system as an instrument for reducing such risks. Middle-class parents are increasingly exercising their market power by investing in educational resources (Brown & Lauder 1992, 20).[13] The organization of the educational system on the basis of a "quasi-market" serves to undermine the postwar commitment to the ideology of meritocracy, where the state sought to restrain the use of the market power of the middle class in order to equalize the opportunity for academic success. In Britain, the existence and dominance of the elite private schools ensured that this commitment was never fully implemented. However, in a market system of education, the ideology of meritocracy is replaced by the ideology of "parentocracy", where the wealth and wishes of parents are given priority over the abilities and efforts of students (Brown 1990). This has involved a major programme of educational reform under the slogans of "choice", "freedom", "standards", and "excellence".[14] The defining feature of the ideology of parentocracy, and the market policies it seeks to legitimate, is not the amount of education received, but the social basis upon which educational selection is organized. An expansion of higher education, for instance, may lead to a larger proportion of working-class students gaining graduate qualifications (assuming that the latter are willing and able to pay off substantial financial debts at the end of their studies), but this does not represent an equalising of opportunities, because certificate holders always stand relative to one another. In Britain, we have argued, the recent increase in graduate numbers will simply mean that differences between institutions of higher learning will increase, rather like the situation in the United States, and the labour market for graduates will become polarized between the "fast-track" leading to senior managerial positions, and a mass of other jobs which offer little in way of career prospects.[15]

These processes of academic and occupational differentiation reflect parallel forces of cultural reproduction whereby social divisions are maintained between those attending the prestigious established universities and those educated in the new universities which may well develop "low status" two-year degree programmes. Through these means, the traditional elites, which have been such a distinctive feature of the British social structure, will be able to transmit their power and privilege intergenerationally (Bourdieu & Passeron 1977).

In the context of the 1990s, the notion that "employers know best", sacrosanct in Conservative policy statements concerning education and training for over a decade, is a curious one, to say the least, in the British context. For over a century, employer commitment to education and training has been derisory when compared to competitor nations (Finegold & Soskice 1990). The idea that employers know what their human resource needs are, and that these can be defined and operationalized in educational terms is unsubstantiated. [16] Employers' "needs" vary enormously; technological innovation ensures that existing knowledge and know-how has a short shelf life, and "short-termism" is endemic:

> few private sector employers plan their recruitment more than 18 months ahead: a third of those who hired new graduates in 1988 were unable to estimate their recruitment needs in the early 1990s.
> " (Department of Education and Science 1990, 56)

It is therefore not surprising to find that universities are suspicious of calls to gear themselves to the needs of industry (Kogan & Kogan 1983). Equally, even on the basis of the limited evidence presented in this book, the early experience of graduates in employment points to a crisis of both morale and motivation, as well as an under-utilization of the skills, talents and capability of highly educated employees.

Changing market conditions resulting from global competition, technological innovation and the creation of quasi-markets in public sector organizations have far-reaching implications for the relationship between higher education and occupational stratification. We have suggested that adaptive organizational structures are being adopted in order to create a more efficient and flexible workforce (Atkinson 1985, Clegg 1990). However, despite the rhetoric associated with the "adaptive" paradigm, in often unintended ways employer selection policies lead to the recruitment of what are defined as "safe bets".

A consequence of this form of social reproduction was clearly understood by John Dewey (1966), who noted that every expansive period of human history is characterized by the operation of forces which "have tended to eliminate distance between peoples and classes previously hemmed off from one another" (p. 100). Hence, a separation into a privileged and a subject-class prevents exposure to an increasing range of contacts, ideas and interests:

> The evils thereby affecting the superior class are less material and less perceptible, but equally real. Their culture tends to be sterile, to be turned back to feed on itself; their art becomes a showy display and artificial; their wealth luxurious; their knowledge over-specialized; their manners fastidious rather than humane . . . Lack of the free and equitable intercourse which springs from a variety of shared interests makes intellectual stimulation unbalanced. Diversity of stimulation means novelty, and novelty means challenge to thought. (Dewey 1966, 98)

In an organizational context, where routine and certainty have been undermined, and where a greater emphasis needs to be placed on innovation and change, new insights and ways of doing things are most likely to spring from bringing together people from diverse educational, occupational and cultural backgrounds.[17] Equally, in uncertain conditions, those in positions of power will seek to maintain their relative advantage even at the expense of economic efficiency. At the heart of the question about organizational change and recruitment is the issue of class, status and power. Social reproduction will, of course, be justified on the basis of objective and meritocratic criteria, but the shift from bureaucratic to adaptive organizational paradigms highlights the importance of social as much as academic qualifications in corporate recruitment processes. In a "low trust" society such as Britain, there seems little prospect of economic innovation by mobilizing highly educated talent, while traditional processes of cultural and social reproduction are able to sustain themselves, despite corporate restructuring, an expansion of higher education, and a predominant ideology which is explicitly meritocratic. Indeed, at the same time as Britain moves towards mass higher education, and the opportunity for social mobility is glimpsed by students who would previously have had little chance of getting into an IHE, traditional bureaucratic careers associated with graduate employment in the past are being undermined.

Notes

1. Whether this will be achieved is another matter. Given a growing deficit in the public sector borrowing requirement (PSBR), the government has

signalled a deceleration in its expansion programme.

2. Presumably so that talent can be utilized regardless of social circumstances. Christopher Ball went on to say, "The employers I have spoken to are ready to see the need to change their recruitment strategies in the 1990s and many have started to do so. There is, of course, a time lag" (p. 756). (See also Ball 1992; CBI 1989; Cassels 1990; Department of Education and Science 1990.)

3. Is this the harbinger of a new age of opportunity and enterprise? It can be objected that in a period of rapid educational and economic change it is impossible to draw conclusive answers to this and other questions raised in this book. This objection is clearly correct, and invites the stock response of any professional academic for "more research". It can also be objected that this study focuses on those who have succeeded in higher education. Therefore, they are all academically successful and do not represent the cohort of young people entering the labour market in the 1990s. However, this should not stop us from drawing together a number of themes which run throughout this study and which may serve to counter the celebratory rhetoric of equity and enterprise.

4. Rather, it is argued that the expansion of higher education reflects credential inflation. As more people gain access to scarce credentials, employers will lift their entry requirements which, in turn, will lead students to demand more advanced courses. As the scarcity value of ever more advanced credentials loses its scarcity value, employers will again raise entry requirements, creating an inflationary spiral (see Dore 1976).

5. Collins extends this analysis by arguing that

Cultural groups based on educational credentials might be regarded as pseudo-ethnic. Not only do they usually originate in the culture of a particular ethnic group and class, but even if widened from that base, they continue to operate to form subjective communities that favour one another in economic dealings and appropriating occupational positions. (Collins 1986, 129).

6. We also argued that the technocratic and social exclusion theories of educational and occupational stratification are not necessarily competing interpretations. It would appear that skill levels have increased, although not for all jobs, and we confront significant problems in defining "skill" precisely because it is a social construct (Dex 1985). Moreover, the scope for human initiative and creativity is often contingent upon the nature of work organization rather than technical competence. Technology is always embedded in a social context, which reflects choices about work organization (Fox 1974).

7. This, of course, also reflects substantial policy changes in industrial relations introduced by the Thatcher/Major Conservative governments. For a comparative analysis, see Lane 1989. Moreover, corporate restruc-

turing has led employers to rethink their recruitment strategies in light of changes in their definitions of managerial and professional competence, as well as codes of organizational control. This has occurred in a context of increasing unemployment and underemployment among all categories of workers.

8. A self-employed consultant or contract worker, for instance, may be more highly "skilled" than those who have retained jobs in the strategic core of medium-sized and large organizations, but can find no shelter from competition in the external labour market (Ashton 1986), which makes them especially vulnerable to business failure, debt or unemployment. This clearly contradicts the idea that performance has become more important than "position" as a determinant of status, salary and career progression (Handy 1989).

9. More also means different in the sense that the university ideal of small-group teaching and intimate tutorial discussions between lecturers engaged in front-line research and half a dozen students is unsustainable, even in the established universities which aped the Oxbridge ideal. As a result, the university lecturer as a cultural model for the student is likely to decline in importance. It is the informal student peer groups that almost exclusively performs this rôle. For working-class students this absence of a cultural "model" is reinforced by the fact that student peer groups tend to be self-selecting on the basis of background, money to participate in certain leisure activities, etc. More importantly, seminar groups of 20 or so students effectively deny students the opportunity to develop their communication and discursive skills in a sustained manner. It is therefore not surprising that the new universities which have the largest staff/student ratios are introducing social and communication skills into the formal curriculum.

10. The elite institutions have argued that resources are being spread too thinly and in order to maintain their research excellence they should receive the lion's share of resources for research.

11. The Vice-Chancellors and Principals (CVCP) who collect and publish these figures need to disaggregate those who drop out of university and the increasing number of students who are changing course, especially given the introduction of modular programmes which should create greater opportunities for students to transfer degrees.

12. This is not achieved by reducing access to welfare, forcing people to make a living by legitimate or illegitimate means. It actually depends upon a well-developed welfare regime. This can only be achieved in societies which have a high tolerance of error, second-chance routes, and a liberal interpretation of talent (Esping-Anderson 1990; Hirschhorn 1984).

13. In a market system of education, material, along with the cultural capital, performs an increasingly important rôle in getting the children from

more privileged backgrounds into "good" schools, as over-subscribed schools choose families who are safe bets when it comes to making a positive contribution to the published examination results, and also willing to make additional financial contributions to the school funds.

14. The new orthodoxy in education is based on an extension of parental choice in a market of competing schools, colleges and universities. Strictly speaking, because education is funded (at least during the compulsory school years) out of the public purse, the idea is to create a quasi-market within which schools will compete. This approximation to the operation of a market is achieved by seeking to create a variety of schools in a mixed economy of public and private institutions. In some cases they will aim at different client groups, such as ethnic minorities, religious sects, or "high flyers". This "variety", it is argued, will provide parents with a genuine choice of different products. Choice of product (type of school) is seen to be sufficient to raise standards for all, because if schools cannot sell enough desk space to be economically viable, they risk going out of business. Therefore, it is assumed that standards will rise because schools that cannot sell enough desk space will be forced to improve their ways in order to attract more customers (parents and students). The argument that the market can lead to greater democratization is particularly evident in the case of higher education. In Britain, there has been a significant increase in the numbers gaining entry to higher education, and the old binary divide between the more "academic" universities and the more "vocational" polytechnics has been abolished, creating a single market for higher education (with some exceptions). Universities now have to compete for both students and research resources. However, whereas higher education has in the past been free to all those with the ability and motivation to benefit from it, students are now having to find a greater proportion of their living costs, although their fees are paid from the public purse. There are also signs that the elite universities will introduce top-up fees to compensate for the declining revenue they receive from the government. The London School of Economics was planning to charge students between £500 and £1,000 on top of the fees which are paid by the state. This was justified in order to maintain academic standards in both teaching and research. Although this proposal has since been rejected, the under-funding of an expansion of higher education in Britain will make the shift towards "private" higher education virtually inevitable.

15. If academic qualifications are to remain a significant determinant of labour market position, then academic performance will always be *relative*, and it is when supply exceeds the demand for labour that the consequences of social inequalities in educational access, and ultimately performance, become most evident. Moreover, if the ideology of parent-

ocracy is important to our understanding of educational selection during the compulsory years at school, it is perhaps going to become even more significant to our understanding of educational selection in further and higher education.

It is also important to note that the ideology of parentocracy has not emerged as a result of a ground swell of popular demand for radical educational reform among a majority of parents, and does not imply an increase in "parent power" over the school curriculum or "choice" of school. On the contrary, it is the state, and not parents that has strengthened its control over what is taught in schools, and it will be schools who choose pupils, rather than parents who choose schools, when it comes to gaining access to more popular educational establishments (Brown 1990).

The shift towards market systems of education has developed against a backdrop of economic recession and high youth unemployment. Neoconservative opponents of "comprehensive" education were not slow to exploit the disquiet expressed by industrialists and felt by middle class parents about the products of the school system. There is no doubt that in this context an escalation in educational expenditure to fund an expansion of higher education and a commitment to strengthen "equality of opportunity" policies have proved difficult to maintain, given that the working-class had not embraced postwar educational reforms as the road to their liberation, and the Left critique of the welfare state in capitalist societies ruled out any possibility that the educational system could improve the life chances of disadvantaged social groups.

16. This is to say nothing of the question of whether the educational system should be subordinated to issues of economic utility.
17. And by incorporating both women and men (which has been shown to have a profound impact on organizational culture; Savage & Witz 1992).

References

Ackroyd, S. 1992. Paradigms lost: paradise regained? In *Rethinking organisation: new directions in organisation theory and analysis*, M. Reed & M. Hughes (eds). London: Sage.

Ainley, B. 1993. *The employment of black and Asian journalists in the British media*. Unpublished PhD thesis, London University.

Ainley, P. 1991. What a performance! Profiling competences as a measure of skill. In *Aspects of vocationalism*. Post-16 Education Centre Occasional Paper No. 2, C. Chitty (ed.). London: Institute of Education.

Ainley, P. 1992. On the trail of the elusive first job. *Guardian*, 1 December.

Ainley, P. 1993. *Class and skill: changing divisions of knowledge and labour*. London: Cassell.

Ainley, P. & S. Vickerstaff forthcoming. Transitions from corporatism: the privatisation of policy failure. *The Journal of Contemporary British History*.

Aldrich, H. J. Cater, T. Jones, D. McEvoy 1981. *Business development and self-segregation: Asian enterprise in three British cities*. London: Croom Helm.

Anderson, C. A. 1962. Access to higher education and economic development. In *Education, economy and society*, A. H. Halsey, J. Floud, C. A. Anderson (eds). Glencoe: Free Press.

Ashton, D. 1986. *Unemployment under capitalism: the sociology of British and American labour markets*. Brighton: Wheatsheaf.

Ashton, D. 1991. Patterns and experience of unemployment. In *Poor work: disadvantage and the division of labour*, P. Brown & R. Scase (eds). Milton Keynes: Open University Press.

Ashton, D. & M. Maguire 1980. The function of academic and non-academic criteria in employers' selection strategies. *British Journal of Guidance and Counselling* **8**(2).

Ashton, D., M. Maguire, M. Spilsbury 1990. *Restructuring the labour market: the implications for youth*. London: Macmillan.

Atkinson J. 1985. The changing corporation. In *New patterns of work*, D.

Clutterbuck (ed.). Aldershot: Gower.

Association of University Teachers (AUT) 1990. *Goodwill under strain: morale in UK universities*. London: AUT.

Bailey, A. 1990. Personal transferable skills for employment: the role of higher education. In *Industry and higher education: collaborating to improve students' learning and training*, P. Wright (ed.). Milton Keynes: Open University Press.

Ball, C. 1990. More means different: wider participation in better higher education. *Journal of the Royal Society of Arts* (RSA), October, 743–57.

Ball, C. 1992. The learning society. *Journal of the Royal Society of Arts*, May, 380–94.

Banks, M., I. Baker, G. Breakwell, J. Bynner, N. Emler, L. Jamieson & K. Roberts 1992. *Careers and identities*. Milton Keynes: Open University Press.

Barnett, C. 1986. *The audit of war: the illusion and reality of Britain as a great nation*. London: Macmillan.

Beck, U. 1992. *Risk society: towards a new modernity*. London: Sage.

Bell, D. 1973. *The coming of post-industrial society*. New York: Basic Books.

Bendix, R. 1956. *Work and authority in industry*. New York: John Wiley.

Bennis, W. 1972. The decline of bureaucracy and organisations of the future. In *Organizational issues in industrial society*, J. M. Shepard (ed.). Englewood Cliffs, New Jersey: Prentice-Hall.

Berg, I. 1970. *Education and jobs: the great training robbery*. New York: Praeger.

Bernstein, B. 1975. *Class, codes and control, vol. 3: towards a theory of educational transmission* (2nd edn). London: Routledge & Kegan Paul.

Best, M. 1990. *The new competition: institutions of industrial restructuring*. Oxford: Polity.

Bills, D. 1988a. Educational credentials and hiring decisions: what employers look for in new employees. *Research in Social Stratification and Mobility* 7, 71–97.

Bills, D. 1988b. Educational credentials and promotions: does schooling do more than get you in the door? *Sociology of Education* 61, 52–60.

Block, F. 1990. *Postindustrial possibilities: a critique of economic discourse*. Berkeley, California: University of California Press.

Boddington, S. 1978. *Science and social action*. London: Allison and Busby.

Bourdieu, P. 1986. *Distinction: a social critique of the judgement of taste*. London: Routledge & Kegan Paul.

Bourdieu, P. 1988. *Homo academicus*. Oxford: Polity.

Bourdieu, P. 1992. Lip service for all at the lycée (translated by D. Robbins). *The Times Higher Education Supplement*, 11 September.

Bourdieu, P. & L. Boltanski 1978. Changes in social structure and changes in the demand for education. In *Contemporary europe: social structure and cultural change*, S. Giner & M. Archer (eds). London: Routledge & Kegan Paul.

Bourdieu, P. & J. Coleman (eds) 1991. *Social theory for a changing society*.

REFERENCES

Boulder, Colorado: Westview Press.

Bourdieu, P. & J. C. Passeron 1964. *The inheritors: French students and their relation to culture.* London: University of Chicago Press.

Bourdieu, P. & J. C. Passeron 1977. *Reproduction in education, society and culture.* London: Sage.

Bourner, T., A. Reynolds, M. Hamed, R. Barnett 1991. *Part-time students and their experience of higher education.* Milton Keynes: SRHE and Open University Press.

Bowles, S. & H. Gintis 1976. *Schooling in capitalist America.* London: Routledge & Kegan Paul.

Boys, C. J., J. Brennan, M. Henkel, J. Kirkland, M. Kogan, P. Youll 1988. *Higher education and the preparation for work.* London: Jessica Kingsley.

Braverman, H. 1974. *Labour and monopoly capital: the degradation of work in the twentieth century.* New York: Monthly Review Press.

Brennan, J. & P. McGeevor 1988. *Graduates at work: degree courses and the labour market.* London: Jessica Kingsley.

Brennan, J. & P. McGeevor 1990. *Ethnic minorities and the graduate labour market.* London: Commission for Racial Equality.

Brown, P. 1987. *Schooling ordinary kids.* London: Tavistock.

Brown, P. 1990. The "third wave": education and the ideology of parentocracy. *British Journal of Sociology of Education* 11(1), 65–85.

Brown, P. & H. Lauder 1992. Education, economy and society: an introduction to a new agenda. In *Education for economic survival: from Fordism to post-Fordism?* P. Brown & H. Lauder (eds). London: Routledge.

Brown, P. & R. Scase 1991. Social change and economic disadvantage in Britain. In *Poor work*, P. Brown & R. Scase (eds). Milton Keynes, Open University Press.

Brown, H. & J. Turbin 1989. *Background and origin of EHE.* Tavistock Institute of Human Relations Working Paper No. 1. Sheffield: Employment Department.

Burrows, R. 1991. The discourse of the enterprise culture and the restructuring of Britain: a polemical contribution. In *Paths of enterprise: the future of the small business*, J. Curran & R. Blackburn (eds). London: Routledge.

Cassels, J. 1990. *Britain's real skill shortage.* London: Policy Studies International.

Chandler, A. D. 1977. *The visible hand: the managerial revolution in American business.* Cambridge, Mass.: Belknap.

Child, J. 1984. *Organization*, 2nd edn. New York: Harper & Row.

Chisholm, L. 1992. A crazy quilt: education, training and social change in Europe. In *Social Europe*, J. Bailey (ed.). London: Longman.

Chitty, C. 1989. *Towards a new education system: the victory of the new right?* London: Falmer.

Clark, B. 1962. *Education and the expert society.* San Francisco: Chandler.

Clegg, S. 1990. *Modern organizations: organization studies in the postmodern world*. London: Sage.

Coffield, F. & R. MacDonald 1991. *Risky business? Youth and the enterprise culture*. London: Falmer.

Collins, R. 1977. Functional and conflict theories of education stratifiction. In *Power and ideology in Education*, J. Karabel & A. H. Halsey (eds) Oxford: Oxford University Press.

Collins, R. 1979. *The credential society: an historical sociology of education and stratification*. New York: Academic.

Collins, R. 1986. *Weberian sociological theory*. Cambridge: Cambridge University Press.

Committee of Vice-Chancellors and Principals (CVCP) 1993. *Review of options for the additional funding of higher education*. London: CVCP.

Confederation of British Industry (CBI) 1989. *Towards a skills revolution*. London: CBI.

Constable, J. & R. McCormick 1987. *The making of British managers: a report for the BIM and the CBI into management training, education and development*. Corby: British Institute of Management.

Council for Industry and Higher Education 1987. *Towards a partnership*. London: Council for Industry and Higher Education.

Crompton, R. & K. Sanderson 1990. *Gendered jobs and social change*. London: Unwin Hyman.

Curran, J. & R. Blackburn (eds) 1991. *Paths of enterprise: the future of the small business*. London: Routledge.

Dale, R. et al. 1990. *The TVEI story: policy, practice and the preparation for the work force*. Milton Keynes: Open University Press.

David, M. 1993. *Parents, gender and education reform*. Oxford: Polity.

Davidson, M. & C. Cooper 1992. *Shattering the glass ceiling*. London: Paul Chapman.

Davies, B. & R. Hare 1989. Explaining the Oxbridge figures. *Oxford Review of Education* 15(3), 221–5.

Department of Education and Science (DES) 1990. *Highly qualified people: supply and demand*. London: HMSO.

Department of Education and Science (DES) 1991. *Higher education: a new framework*. London: HMSO.

Department of Employment (DoE) 1992. Economic activity and qualifications. *Employment Gazette* 100, 101–33.

Department of Employment (DoE) 1993. Ethnic origins and the labour market. *Employment Gazette* 101(2), 25–43.

Devine, F. 1992. Gender segregation in the engineering and science professions: a case of continuity and change. *Work, Employment and Society* 6(4), 557–75.

Dewey, J. 1966. *Democracy and education*. New York: Free Press.

REFERENCES

Dex, S. 1985. *The sexual division of work*. Brighton: Wheatsheaf.

Dore, R. 1976. *The diploma disease*. London: Allen & Unwin.

Esping-Andersen, G. 1990. *The three worlds of welfare capitalism*. Oxford: Polity.

Evans, C. 1993. *English people: the experience of teaching and learning English in British universities*. Milton Keynes: Open University Press.

Fallows, J. 1985. The case against credentialism. *The Atlantic Review*, December, 49–67.

Fevre, R. 1992. *The sociology of labour markets*. Hemel Hempstead: Harvester Wheatsheaf.

Finch, J. 1983. *Married to the job*. London: Allen & Unwin.

Finegold, D., E. Keep, D. Miliband, D. Robertson, K. Sisson, J. Ziman 1992. *Higher education: expansion and reform*. London: Institute for Public Policy Research.

Finegold, D. & D. Soskice 1990. The failure of training in Britain: analysis and prescription. In *Education, training and employment: educated labour – the changing basis of industrial demand*, G. Esland (ed.). Wokingham: Addison-Wesley.

Finn, D. 1987. *Training without jobs: new deals and broken promises*. London: Macmillan.

Fisher, I. 1927. *The nature of capital and income*. London: Macmillan.

Fox, A. 1974. *Beyond contract: work, power and trust relations*. London: Faber and Faber.

Fromm, E. 1949. *Man for himself: an enquiry into the psychology of ethics*. London: Routledge & Kegan Paul.

Fromm, E. 1962. Personality and the market place. In *Man, work and society*, S. Nosow & W. Form (eds). New York: Basic Books.

Fulton, O. 1991. Slouching towards a mass system: society, government and institutions in the United Kingdom. *Higher Education* 21, 589–605.

Gallie, D. 1991. Patterns of skill change: upskilling, deskilling or the polarization of skills? *Work, Employment and Society* 5(3), 319–51.

Gamble, A. 1988. *The free economy and the strong state: the politics of Thatcherism*. London: Macmillan.

Gergen, K. 1992. Organisation theory in the postmodern era. In *Rethinking organisation: new directions in organisation theory and analysis*, M. Reed & M. Hughes (eds). London: Sage.

Giddens, A. 1991. *Modernity and self-Identity: self and society in the late modern age*. Oxford: Polity.

Ginzberg, E. 1966. *The development of human resources*. New York: McGraw-Hill.

Glass, D. 1959. Education and social change in modern England. In *Law and opinion in England in the twentieth century*, M. Ginsberg (ed.). London: Stevens and Son.

Gordon, A. 1983. Attitudes of employers to the recruitment of graduates.

Educational Studies **9**(1), 45–64.

Gramsci, A. 1971. *Selections from the prison notes of Antonio Gramsci*. London: Lawrence and Wishart.

Granovetter, M. 1974. *Getting a job: a study of contacts and careers*. Cambridge, Mass.: Harvard University Press.

Green, A. 1990. *Education and state formation: the rise of education systems in England, France and the* USA. London: Macmillan.

Greenhalgh, C. 1989. *Employment and structural change in Britain: trends and policy options*. London. Employment Institute.

Hague, D. 1991. *Beyond universities: a new republic of the intellect*. Hobart paper 115. London: Institute of Economic Affairs.

Hall, S. & M. Jacques (eds) 1989. *New times: the changing face of politics in the 1990s*. London: Lawrence and Wishart.

Halsey, A. H. 1962. The changing functions of universities. In *Education, economy and society*, A. H. Halsey, J. Floud, C. A. Anderson (eds). Glencoe: Free Press.

Halsey, A. H. 1992a. *Decline of donnish dominion: the British academic professions in the twentieth century*. Oxford: Clarendon.

Halsey, A. H. 1992b. *Opening Wide the Doors of Higher Education*. National Commission on Education Briefing No. 6, August. London: National Commission on Education.

Halsey, A. H. & M. Trow 1971. *The British academics*. Cambridge, Mass.: Harvard University Press.

Handy, C. 1985. *Gods of management*. London: Pan.

Handy, C. 1987. *The making of managers: a report on management education, training and development in the* USA, *West Germany, France, Japan and the UK*. London: National Economic Development Office.

Handy, C. 1989. *The age of unreason*. London: Business Books.

Harvey, D. 1989. *The conditions of postmodernity: an enquiry into the origins of cultural change*. Oxford: Blackwell.

Haviland, J. 1988. *Take care, Mr Baker!: the advice on education reform which the government collected but withheld*. London: Fourth Estate.

Herriot, P. 1984. *Down from the ivory tower: graduates and their jobs*. Chichester: John Wiley.

Hirsch, F. 1977. *Social limits to growth*. London: Routledge & Kegan Paul.

Hirschhorn, L. 1984. *Beyond mechanization: work and technology in a post-industrial age*. Cambridge, Mass.: MIT Press.

Hobsbawm, E. 1969. *Industry and empire*. London: Pelican.

Hofstede, G. 1991. *Culture and organisation*. London: McGraw-Hill.

Hughes, E. 1958. *Men and their work*. Glencoe: Free Press.

Jackson, B. & D. Marsden 1966. *Education and the working class*. Harmondsworth: Penguin.

Jenkins, R. 1985. Black workers in the labour market: the price of recession.

REFERENCES

In *New approaches to economic life*, B. Roberts, R. Finnegan & D. Gallie (eds.) Manchester: Manchester University Press.

Jenkins, R. 1992. *Pierre Bourdieu*. London: Routledge.

Jessup, G. 1991. *Outcomes: NVQs and the emerging model of education and training*. London: Falmer.

Jones, A. 1990. A responsive higher education system. In *Industry and higher education: collaboration to improve students' learning and training*, P. Wright (ed.). Milton Keynes: SHRE and Open University Press.

Jones, G. & C. Wallace 1992. *Youth, family and citizenship*. Milton Keynes: Open University Press.

Jones, K. 1989. *Right turn: the conservative revolution in education*. London: Hutchinson Radius.

Kanter, R. 1984. *The change masters*. London: Allen & Unwin.

Kanter, R. 1989. *When giants learn to dance*. London: Simon and Schuster.

Kanter, R. 1991. The future of bureaucracy and hierarchy in organisational theory: a report from the field. In *Social theory for a changing society*, P. Bourdieu & J. S. Coleman (eds). Boulder, Colorado: Westview.

Kelsall, R., A. Poole, A. Kuhn 1972. *Graduates: the sociology of an elite*. London: Methuen.

Keniston, K. 1965. *The uncommitted: alienated youth in American society*. New York: Delta.

Kerr, C., J. Dunlop, F. Harbison, C. Myers 1973. *Industrialism and industrial man*. Harmondsworth: Penguin.

Kogan, M. with D. Kogan 1983. *The attack on higher education*. London: Kogan Page.

Krieger, J. 1986. *Reagan, Thatcher and the politics of decline*. Oxford: Polity.

Kuhn, T. 1962. *The structure of scientific revolutions*. Chicago: University of Chicago Press.

Kumar, K. 1989. The limits and divisions of industrial capitalism. In *Industrial societies: crisis and division in western capitalism and state socialism*, R. Scase (ed.). London: Unwin Hyman.

Laborit, H. 1977. *Decoding the human message*. London: Allison and Busby.

Landes, D. 1968. *The unbound Prometheus: technological change and industrial development in Western Europe from 1750 to the present*. Cambridge: Cambridge University Press.

Lane, C. 1989. *Management and labour in Europe*. Aldershot: Edward Elgar.

Larson, M. 1977. *The rise of professionalism: a sociological analysis*. California: University of California Press.

Lash, S. & J. Urry 1987. *The end of organised capitalism*. Oxford: Polity.

Lowe, R. 1990. Educating for industry: the historical role of higher education in England. In *Industry and higher education: collaboration to improve students' learning and training*, P. Wright (ed.). Milton Keynes: Open University Press.

Maclure, J. 1968. *Education documents: England and Wales 1816–1968*. London: Methuen.

Marshall, A. 1920. *Principles of economics: an introductory volume*. London: Macmillan.

Marshall, T. H. 1963. *Sociology at a crossroads and other essays*. London: Heinemann.

McGregor, D. 1960. *The human side of enterprise*. New York: McGraw-Hill.

Merton, R. K. 1964. *Social theory and social structure*. Glencoe: Free Press.

Minkes, A. 1987. *The entrepreneurial manager*. Harmondsworth: Penguin.

Minzberg, H. 1983. *Structures in fives: designing effective organisations*. Englewood Cliffs, New Jersey: Prentice Hall.

Murphy, R. 1988. *Social closure: the theory of monopolization and exclusion*. Oxford: Clarendon.

Newman, J. 1943. *On the scope and nature of university education*. London: Everyman.

Nicholson, N. & M. West 1988. *Managerial job change: men and women in transition*. Cambridge: Cambridge University Press.

Nuttgens, P. 1988. *What should we teach and how should we teach it?: Aims and purposes of higher education*. Aldershot: Wildwood House.

OECD 1989. *Education and the economy in a changing society*. Paris: Organization for Economic Co-operation and Development.

Offe, C. 1976. *Industry and inequality*. London: Edward Arnold.

Overbeek, H. 1990. *Global capitalism and national decline: the Thatcher decade in perspective*. London: Unwin Hyman.

Pahl, J. & R. Pahl 1971. *Managers and their wives*. Harmondsworth: Penguin.

Parkin, F. 1979. *Marxism and class theory: a bourgeois critique*. London: Tavistock.

Parsons, T. 1959. The school class as a social system: some of its functions in American society. Harvard Educational Review, **XXIX**, 297–318.

Pearson, R. & G. Pike 1989. *The graduate labour market in the 1990s*. Falmer, Sussex: Institute of Manpower Studies.

Perkin, H. 1989. *The rise of professional society: England since 1880*. London: Routledge.

Peters, T. 1992. *Liberation management*. London: Macmillan.

Peters, T. & R. Waterman 1982. *In search of excellence*. New York: Harper & Row.

Porter, M. 1990. *The competitive advantage of nations*. London: Macmillan.

Reed, M. & M. Hughes (eds) 1992. *Rethinking organisation: new directions in organisation theory and analysis*. London: Sage.

Robbins, D. 1991. *The work of Pierre Bourdieu*. Milton Keynes: Open University Press.

Robinson, E. 1968. *The new polytechnics*. Harmondsworth: Penguin.

Roizen, J. & M. Jepson 1985. *Degrees for jobs: employer expectations of higher education*. Guildford: SHRE and NFER–Nelson.

Rudd, E. 1984. A comparison between the results achieved by women and men studying for first degrees in British universities. *Studies in Higher Education* **9**(1) 45–7.

Ryle, G. 1963. *The concept of mind*. Harmondsworth: Penguin.

Sabel, C. 1982. *Work and politics: the division of labour in industry*. Cambridge: Cambridge University Press.

Salter, B. & T. Tapper 1992. *Oxford, Cambridge and the changing idea of the university: the challenge to donnish domination*. Milton Keynes: Open University Press.

Sanderson, M. 1972. *The universities and British industry, 1850–1970*. Cambridge: Cambridge University Press.

Savage, M. & A. Witz (eds) 1992. *Gender and bureaucracy*. Oxford: Blackwell.

Scase, R. 1992. *Class*. Milton Keynes: Open University Press.

Scase, R. & R. Goffee 1989. *Reluctant managers: their work and life styles*. London: Routledge.

Schein, E. 1985. *Organizational culture and leadership*. London: Jossey Bass.

Schuller, T. (ed.) 1991. *The future of higher education*. Milton Keynes: SHRE and Open University Press.

Schultz, T. 1960. Capital formation by education. *Journal of Political Economy* **68**, 571–83.

Schultz, T. 1961. Investment in human capital. *American Economic Review* **51**, 1–17.

Schultz, T. W. 1968. Human Capital. *International encyclopedia of the social sciences*, **2**, 278–87.

Schumpeter, J. 1976. *Capitalism, socialism and democracy*. London: Allen & Unwin.

Scott, J. 1991. *Who rules Britain?* Oxford: Polity.

Scott, P. 1992. Editorial. *The Times Higher Education Supplement*, 21 August.

Sennett, R. & Cobb, J. 1977. *The hidden injuries of class*. Cambridge: Cambridge University Press.

Shils, E. 1958. The concentration and dispersion of charisma: their bearing on economic policy in underdeveloped countries. *World Politics* **11**, 1–19.

Shils, E. 1965. Charisma, order and status. *American Sociological Review* **30**, 199–213.

Shils, E. 1968. Charisma. *International encyclopedia of the social sciences* **2**, 286–390.

Silver, H. & J. Brennan 1988. *A liberal vocationalism*. London: Methuen.

Simmel, G. 1978. *The philosophy of money* (edited by D. Frisby). London: Routledge & Kegan Paul.

Smith, V. 1990. *Managing in the corporate interest*. Berkeley, California: University of California Press.

Stanley, M. 1978. *The technological conscience: survival and dignity in an age of expertise*. New York: Free Press.

Stanworth, P. & A. Giddens 1974. *Elites and power in British society*. Cambridge: Cambridge University Press.

Statham, J, D. Mackinnon, H. Cathcard, M. Hales 1991. *The education factfile: a handbook on education information in the UK*, 2nd edn. Sevenoaks, London: Hodder & Stoughton.

Stephens, M. (ed.) 1989. *Universities, education and the national economy*. London: Routledge.

Tarsh, J. 1990. Graduate employment and degree class. *Employment Gazette*, October, 489–99.

Tawney, R. 1982. *The acquisitive society*. Brighton: Wheatsheaf.

Thomas, K. 1990. *Gender and subject in higher education*. Milton Keynes: Open University Press.

Tight, M. 1991. *Higher education: a part-time perspective*. Milton Keynes: SHRE and Open University Press.

Turner, R. H. 1960. Sponsored and contest mobility and the school system. *American Sociological Review* **25**, 855–67.

Vaizey, J. 1962. *Education for tomorrow*. Harmondsworth: Penguin.

Wakeford, J. 1969. *The cloistered elite: a sociological analysis of the English public boarding school*. London: Macmillan.

Walby, S. 1986. *Patriarchy at work: patriarchal and capitalist relations in employment 1800–1984*. Oxford: Polity.

Wallerstein, I. 1979. *The capitalist world-economy*. Cambridge: Cambridge University Press.

Ward, R. & M. Cross 1991. Race, employment and economic change. In *Poor work: disadvantage and the division of labour*, P. Brown & R. Scase (eds). Milton Keynes: Open University Press.

Weber, M. 1978. *Economy and society*, G. Roth & C. Wittich (eds). Berkeley, California: University of California Press.

Whyte, W. 1965. *The organization man*. Harmondsworth: Penguin.

Wiener, M. 1981. *English culture and the decline of the industrial spirit 1850–1980*. Cambridge: Cambridge University Press.

Wilensky, H. 1962. Careers, life styles and social integration. In *Man, work and society*, S. Nosow & W. H. Form (eds). New York: Basic Books.

Wilson, R. M. 1989. *Ripley Bogle*. London: Pan.

Witz, A. 1992. *Professions and patriarchy*. London: Routledge.

Wolin, S. 1961. *Politics and vision*. London: Allen & Unwin.

Wright, E. 1984. A general framework for the analysis of class structure. In *The debate on classes*, E. Wright (ed.). London: Verso.

Young, M. & P. Willmott 1973. *The symmetrical family: a study of work and leisure in the London region*. London: Routledge.

Zuboff, S. 1989. *In the age of the smart machine: the future of work and power*. Oxford: Heinemann.

Index

academic drift   34
academic hierarchy   47, 168
  effects of location in   71–2
academic performance, relative   178–9n
academic credentials   16–18, 25–6,
  30n, 143
acceptability   130–33, 140, 143
  black job seekers disadvantaged
  130–31
adaptive (flexible) organization   9, 10,
  11, 21, 119–20
  acceptability   131–2
  administration "down–sized"   150
  career prospects uncertain in   147
  desirable personal attributes   12
  "disadvantaged" groups   23–4
  leadership skills within   10–11
  mutual compatibility   142–3
  performance-related payment   150
  selection for fast-tracking   125–6
  shift towards   12, 13, 19, 20, 21–2,
  175
  work/personal lives division   167
administration   3
anti-industrial bias   170–71
aristocracy, and the industrial revolution   32
Asian students, preference for
  traditional bureaucratic careers   95
assessment   140–42, 170
assessment centres   140–41, 142
attitudes, conformist   89–90, 92–3
  entrepreneurial   90, 104–8, 170–71

flexible   89–9, 99–104, 113
  traditional bureaucratic   89, 93–9
attitudes, non-conformist   90–2
  drop-out   90–91, 108–9
  ritualist   91, 109–10
  socially committed   91–2, 110–12

British culture, nature of   12
bureaucracy   2–4, 7
bureaucratic
  career, traditional   93–9, 175
    and career–family conflict   95–6
  organization   2–4, 86, 91
    assignment of tasks within   19–20
    loss of middle managers/supervisers
    144
  paradigm   5–7
    demise of   6–7
  personality   19–20
  work, demise of   166
bureaucratic–adaptive organization
  shift   19, 20, 21–2, 175
business ownership, tradition in Asian
  community   105–106
business start-up, attractive   158–60
business studies, demand for   26

capability   118, 125–30, 143
  key elements of criteria   127–30
capital   28
  material
    conversion to cultural capital   42,
    143

and education   177–8n
potential sources of   31n
see also cultural capital
career paths   162, 167
career portfolios
  building of   99, 102–103
  and social confidence   103–104
career–private relationships   96–7
careers
  career structures   93–4, 95
  expectations dampened   152
  long–term, not expected   154–5
  non-conventional   170–71
  opportunities restricted   150
  perspectives more pragmatic and
    flexible   147
  and ritualist attitudes   91
  seen as source of personal motiva-
    tion   148–9
  traditional bureaucratic   95, 167
    avoided by "flexible" students
    100–101
charisma   43, 124–5, 172
charismatic leadership   10, 11, 12, 24
charismatic personality   19, 127–9,
  157, 169–70
  and managerial qualities   21
child-bearing, and female exclusion   160–61
class divisions   147, 162–3
class status   55, 175
class structure, social reproduction
  of   116, 174–5
cognitive management   4
compatibility   22, 130, 172
competitive advantage
  Japan and Pacific Rim countries   39
  small/medium–sized companies   8
contest mobility   35–6
contracts, fixed-term   88
corporate dependency, avoidance of
  100
corporate leaders, values, attitudes and
  beliefs   12–13
corporate restructuring   6, 19, 176–7n
  and graduate recruitment   51
  welcomed by "flexible" students
    100–101
cost effective pressures   5–6

credentials   168
  credential inflation   176n
  importance of increased   137
  now convey insufficient informa-
    tion   138–9
  see also academic credentials
credentials–skills–class structure link
  166
"cult of the grade"   55–7
cultural barriers, and recruitment
  156–7
cultural capital   28–9, 31n, 162, 172
  appropriate   27, 147
  growing significance of   19
  middle-class   27, 43, 140, 141–2
  and personal/social skills   132–3
  purchasing power of   143
  and social confidence   60–62
cultural code, and entry to managerial
  jobs   22
cultural groups, pseudo-ethnic   176n
cultural identity, and life-style   141–2
cultural knowledge   83n
cultural reproduction   173–4

"de-layering"   150, 166–7
decision-making, open-participative
  approach   10
degrees   60, 103
  need for   27, 134, 138
demarcation, gendered   28–9
disadvantaged groups   12, 23–4
  less room at the top for   172
discrimination   95
  in selection/promotion   43
distance learning, Open University   36
down-sizing   87, 150, 166

economic restructuring   26
education   15, 27, 173, 178n
  by "followership"   24
  compensatory   170
  "comprehensive", disquiet concern-
    ing   179n
  credentials vs. personal/social
    skills   24
  as a form of investment   15–16
  marketization of   140, 179n
  and occupational structure   164

power of 67
private
  advantage of 103
  shift to free market systems 173
education system 4, 15, 25, 31*n*
  complaints reflect needs of recruiters 22
  screening out of unsuitable candidates 133
education–credentials–class divisions
link, changed 169–70
education–employment–social class,
changing relationships of 172
education–labour market contradiction 19
education–occupational stratification
relationship 19, 167
  and changing market conditions
  174
  power struggle for scarce credentials 165–6
  social exclusion theory 17–18, 30*n*,
  165, 176n
  technocratic theory 16–17, 18, 28,
  165, 166, 176*n*
effortless achievement 55, 79, 83*n*
elites
  cultural code of 22
  and higher education 38–9
  traditional 173–4
employers 50, 174
  may raise entry requirements 168
  and Oxbridge recruits 73–4
  preferences 79–80
  recruitment strategies 116–45
  and status of credentials 168
  use of short-term contracts 140
employing organizations 148, 150
  seen as non-meritocratic 155–6
employment relationship, de-collectiv-
ized 87–8
enterprise 171
Enterprise in Higher Education
Initiative (EHEI) 11, 14n
entrepreneurial vs. professionalized
society 171–2
entrepreneurship 87, 158, 170, 171
  appeal of 159–60
equal opportunities, and possible

decline in standards 134
ethnic divisions 162–3
ethnic minorities
  in higher education 37–8
  lacking at Oxbridge 74
  in universities 74–5
examination success, important 56–7
exclusions, damaging to international
competitiveness 164–5
expectation, unmet 51
expert knowledge base, important
121

fast-track graduate training programmes 25, 27, 50, 113, 137, 168,
173
  access for lower socio–economic
  groups unlikely 170
  greater importance of 166–7
fees and loans 41
Fordism 2–3, 38–9
free market, and educational finance
40
funding system, higher education 42

gender 83*n*
  gender divisions 162–3
  inequalities narrowing 37
  and student assessment of academic
  attainment 57
gender relations, middle-class 149–54
geographical mobility, and careers
149
Graduate Enterprise Scheme 88
graduate qualification *see* degrees
graduate recruiters *see* recruiters
graduate recruitment *see* recruitment
graduate training programmes 127
  purposes of 157–8
graduates 113, 134, 162
  in employment 146–63
    expect to retain present jobs 167–
    8
  encouraged to be more independent
  and self–reliant 88
  enterprising 170–1
  female
    felt disadvantaged 160–2
    thought to lack leadership poten-

tial 161
pragmatic approach to employment 147–8, 162
some more equal than others 135–
7, 168

"hidden injuries of class" 61–2
higher education 15, 16, 35, 41, 47,
65, 165
and bureaucratic organization 38–9
expansion of 16, 33, 53n, 164, 173
official justification for 39–40
results of 168
underfunded 178n
extension of 44–5
gives working–class students a
choice 68–9
lecturers teach to requirements of
professional bodies 114n
"more" means "different" 41
reform and expansion of 29–30
single market for 40, 178n
social class inequalities 36–8
a status–confirming activity 170
Higher Education Enterprise Initiative 88, 89
higher education–graduate careers
relationship, changes in 47
hiring criteria 145n
home background, student 86–7
"Home Counties" students
appreciation of developed cognitive
capacity 66–7
attitudes of 48–9
aware of place in higher education
hierarchy 78–9
with "flexible" orientation 113
lack of ethnic minorities 74
personal/transferable skills gained
64
home-work distinction 151–2
human capital/resources 116–18, 164
change in recruiters' thinking
116–18
increased importance of 16

individual assessment 39
Industrial Revolution 52n
industry-education links 139

information systems, computer-
based 6
information technology 150
"Inner City" students 64
appreciation of developed cognitive
capacity 66
attitudes 49, 50
and course worth 81
few with "flexible approach" 104
understood place in education/
employment hierarchy 80–2
Institutions of Higher Education
(IHEs) 2, 4, 5, 19, 170
instrumentalism 26
intellectual achievement, accumulation
of 58–9
intelligence 127
interpersonal skills 22, 132, 162
intrapreneurship 7, 171

job satisfaction 94
job screening, intensification of 168
job security 6, 95, 97, 110
under threat 87, 98–9, 166
jobs, temporary, low-skilled 90–91
junior management 4, 27

knowledge–application contradiction
46

labour force 18–19
labour market 16
graduate, becoming polarized 173
student orientation to 112
students' cognitive map 75–6
leadership 10–11, 124–5, 161
local government services 118
London School of Economics 41–2

management consultancy 102,
170–71
management development 11–12
management information systems 150
management science 3
managers 3, 6
central importance of work 148–9
more pragmatic approach to employers 150–52
and rôle allocation 3–4

market power
of middle class parents 173
and occupational success 27–8
Masters in Business Administration
(MBA) 134–5
mature students 60, 64
working-class 79
media, marketing and advertising,
attraction of 115n
meritocracy 16–17, 28, 173
middle class(es) 5, 14n, 29
and cultural capital 27, 140, 141–2,
143
and cultural heritage 33–4
demand for academic credentials
25–6
exertion of market power 173
path into 95
university–economy relationship 33
middle management 4, 27
motor industry, increased technical
competence 122

networking 156–7
by students 103
"Old Boys Network" 73–4
universities–employing organizations 139–40
works against women 160
niche marketing 6
non-academic qualities 25

occupational careers 92–3, 94–5, 98,
101
in construction of incremental career
portfolios 99
desired by female students 96–7
occupational insecurity 166
oil crisis (1973) 5
organizational change 1–2, 154
organizational cultures 7–8
organizational effectiveness 8
organizational paradigms, changing
19, 20
organizational restructuring 2, 6, 13,
19, 30–31n
organizations, large–scale 1, 2, 8, 160
class relationships, social mobility and
IHEs 4–5

inhibiting risk-taking 87
"matrices" and "adhocracies" 8
Oxbridge 44, 52n, 54n, 135, 147
intense competition at 57
legacy of domination 34
recruitment from 33
Oxbridge graduates
advantageous position of 156–7
optimism about career chances 152
preference for 75–7, 168
Oxbridge students 63–4
attitudes of 47–8, 49
awareness of employer demands 73
competitive edge 60
"flexible" approach 104, 113
on Oxbridge students 71–2

Pacific Rim countries 5, 39
paradigm, notion of 13n
parentocracy, ideology of 173,
178–9n
parents
aspirations rising 34
middle-class, conversion of material
to cultural capital 143
pressure, and university choice 79
partners, and their careers 104
perceptions 50, 51
instrumental 90
personal freedom and initiative 106
personal qualities 11, 29, 43
charismatic 169–70
personal relationships 153
rôle of work within 154
personal skills 130
flexible 122–4
personal/social skills training 11
personal/transferable skills 42–3, 64,
116, 118, 119
acquired by working-class students
63
need for 154–5
taught, new universities 43–4
"personality package" 22–3
polytechnics 35, 36, 40
private enterprise, and minority
groups 107
privatization, seen as worrying 98
profession, defined 114n

"professional mystique" 114–15*n*
professionalized society 171–2
professions
  exclusion from 18, 33
  security seen to be undermined 98
psychological contract, redefinitions
  of 150–52, 162
public service, cash nexus in 98

qualifications, and changing nature of
  professional/mangerial work 25

recession 144, 162, 179*n*
recruiters 12, 24, 50, 116–18
  paying more attention to "personal-
    ity" 139
  recruitment and the recruited 116
  search for future leaders 125–7
  selection of applicants 135
recruitment 4, 140–41
  employer shift in criteria of 130
  informal 74
  polarization in 167
  targeting of 139–40
recruitment strategies 176–7*n*
  graduate hierarchy 135–7
recruits 140
  increase in potential pool of 135
"risk" society 172
Robbins Report 35
rôle cultures 9–10

"safe bets" 23, 29, 144, 174
schools, and learning 17
schools/universities, and bureaucratic
  principles 88–9
scientific management *see* Fordism
scientific/technical training 34
selection, meritocratic 35
selection process 118–33
  acceptability 130–33
  capability 118, 125–30
  suitability 119–25
self–employment 88, 90, 107–108,
  177*n*
senior management 9, 24, 32
  choosing compatible candidates 162
  fast-track programme for 167
  from elite universities 4

and entrepreneurship 7
  introduction of adaptive (flexible)
    organization 10
  manipulating personal networks 156
  and staff control 10–11
short–term goals 147
"short–termism" 174
single market, higher education 40
skills
  in demand 120–21
  and modular study 43
  skill levels 17, 18
skills courses, teaching-only institutions 41
small business start-up 88
  see also business start-up
small businesses 104–105
  set up by women 161–2
social confidence 62, 172
  and career portfolio construc-
    tion 103–104
  and cultural capital 60–62
social divisions, maintained 173–4
"social fit" 130
social inequalities, and job selection
  137
social mobility
  "sponsored or contest" 35–6
  working-class 26
social qualifications 169–70, 175
social reproduction 116, 174–5
socialization, and career success 149
sociological research, fragmented 2
sponsored mobility 36
sponsorship 139
  and patronage 162
student attitudes survey 47–51
student unrest 45
student–business links 103
students 2, 40–41, 69–70
  absolute increase in 36–7
  aware of social differentiation 71
  difficulties of classifying 70–71
  disadvantaged 49
  ethnic minority 50, 95
  failing to complete studies 169
  female 50, 134
    labour market discrimination 75
    solution of career-family conflict

95–6
want occupational careers   96–7
middle-class   49, 59–60
   "payment for privilege"   169
   possessing personal qualities   44
non-conformist   108–109
non-Oxbridge, complaints of lack of
   meritocratic selection   77–8
orientations to work and careers
   86–115
part-time   49
perceptions of   50, 51
predominently conformist perspective   112–13
"socially-committed"   110–12
working-class   36, 63, 173
   absence of cultural model   177n
   acquisition of middle-class habits
   67–8
   and cultural capital   19, 143
   mature   97–8
   and social confidence   60–62
   traditional bureaucratic careers   95
study subjects, considered irrelevant
   63
suitability   119–25, 143
suitability/acceptability distinction
   118

talent
   better use of   164, 176n
   wastage of   165
teams/team work   123–4
   and team players   131
technical colleges   36
technical competence   119, 121–2,
   130
technical skills, importance of   23
technological innovation   174
technology, new   18–19, 63
top-up fees   41–2, 169, 178n
training
   of minds   65–6
   to handle change   117
trust, culture of   149

under-representation, of women and
   ethnic minorities   133
unemployment   39, 87

graduate   45, 46, 167–8, 172
universities   26, 68, 71–2, 169
   elite   4, 44, 47, 48, 178n
   established   14n, 44, 47, 57, 147,
   168
   flexibly oriented, students better
      prepared for work   147
   increasing differentiation   168–9
   more vocationally-oriented   11
   new   14n, 47, 135–6
      foundation of   35
      introducing social and communica-
         tions skills   170, 177n
      students of lesser calibre   136–7
   reliance on state funding   52–3n
   sheltered life at   64–5
   student population   35–6
   top ten   44, 45
   Victorian civic foundations   34
universities–graduate employers, closer
   links   11
university staff, short–term contracts
   113n
university tradition, two major
   models   55
upward mobility   36, 95

vocational relevance, higher education   30, 46
vocationalism, liberal   36

women   95, 133
   as managers (a view)   112
   setting up small businesses   161–2
   in university education   37
   wishing to develop own talents/
      skills   151
work, location within general life-
   style   151–4
work experience, present jobs considered to be   147–8
work placement   139
work rôles, and specific objectives   7
workers, flexible and adaptable   22
working class, defined   14n
working life
   disillusionment with   147
   transition to   146